THE
CRYSTAL
YEAR

THE
CRYSTAL
YEAR

CRYSTAL WISDOM
THROUGH THE SEASONS

CLAIRE TITMUS

Illustrated by Anastasia Stefurak

Photography by India Hobson

Hardie Grant

QUADRILLE

THE CRYSTAL YEAR

CRYSTAL GUIDE AND MOON KNOWLEDGE 164

COSMIC WELCOMES

Hello, you beautiful soul. Chances are you've discovered this book by chance, by fate, or because a friend has recommended it to you. Either way, we are glad you are here (and by 'we', I mean me, Claire, the crystals and the book).

You may be a beginner or you may be a crystal connoisseur, but whatever your experience, think back to the first time you held, saw or were gifted a crystal. What was it? Do you still have it? At the moment you encountered your first crystal, you embarked upon a magical, spiritual crystal journey and opened your divine energies to a higher plane. You may not have been aware of it, but the crystal would have been vibrating at such a high level that your chakras, spiritual energy and aura would have reacted, working for you and with you to align you.

As we make our way through the year together, you will be introduced to many different crystals, all of which can be used to suit many different needs or life situations. The ones listed within the chapters, directory and beyond are commonly found crystals, to ensure you can find them with ease – you may even already have some of them in your collection.

I can't wait to guide you on this journey to discovering the magic of crystals, the seasons, some popular festivals and celebrations, and so much more. Over the next 12 chapters, we will explore how to choose the best crystals to support your needs, how to care for your crystals, and how to live with spiritual awareness. So, open your mind to the possibilities and let's start this journey together.

Love and light,

Claire

AN INTRODUCTION TO CRYSTALS

Before we start, let's briefly talk about what crystals are.

Crystals, rocks, gemstones – whatever you wish to call them – are gifted to us by Mother Nature. The fact that these treasures even exist is a miracle of magic and science. Incredible processes within the Earth have brought them to life over thousands of years.

In scientific terms, crystals are formed by the crystallization of cooling magma, the evaporation of salt water, and the cooling and hardening of water. As they slowly grow and form, they trap energies from different eras, across an expanse of time. Once formed, crystals remain filled with atomic, molecular and spiritual energy. It is said that this incredible energy, which vibrates from within the crystal's molecules, works with our own life energy, providing us with support, as well as physical, mental and spiritual healing. Pretty amazing, if you ask me!

So, which crystals can help you? I want to make it clear that, while I suggest specific crystals for certain ailments and chakras throughout the book, trusting your intuition is essential when making a choice – and your individual choices and decisions are so important.

Think about what you are attracted to, what gives you happy vibes, what gives you that 'feeling'. If a crystal jumps out at you, there is often a subconscious reason. It has chosen you. Try it now: if you own more than one crystal, close your eyes and let your intuition decide which one is going to support you today. Now look up the description in the Popular Crystals Directory (pages 165–172), and you may be surprised by how much its meaning resonates with exactly what you need right now. Spooky, right?!

Remember, don't overcomplicate or overthink the process of working with crystals; with so many available sources for learning about these precious stones, you'll come into contact with a wealth of information as you embark on your spiritual path. There's no need to feel overwhelmed: go with what's right for you. The more positive and relaxed you feel, the more open you'll be to receiving what you need, and the more freely the universe will respond to you.

HOW TO USE CRYSTALS

Just as you would use your intuition when choosing crystals, listen to yourself when deciding how to use them for your highest good.

Here are a few general guidelines to get you started.

1. Keep a bag of your favourite crystals with you at all times. When you need support, take out the crystal you need and hold it for a few moments. Tumbles work well for this (see page 175).

2. Use crystals during meditation or yoga, especially when you want to reach a deeper level of relaxation or connect with guidance. See the Sun Meditation Ritual on page 80.

3. Take a bath with your **quartz** crystals (such as **clear quartz, rose quartz** and **amethyst**). If they're water-safe (see the Popular Crystals Directory on pages 165–172 or the list on page 180), feel free place them in the water with you. If they're not water-safe, placing them on the edge of the bath with candles and flowers is a relaxing alternative.

4. Use crystals according to their properties: for example, carry a crystal for wealth or good fortune in your purse or wallet, or place a crystal for sleep or fertility under your pillow.

5. Place crystals around your plants. This can be beneficial for both your own wellbeing and your plants' health.

6. Wear crystal bracelets – on your left wrist to receive energy from the crystal, or on your right to allow the crystal's energy to flow out into the environment.

7. Wear a crystal necklace, especially if you have chosen a crystal that supports the heart, throat or third-eye chakras. You'll find this information in the Popular Crystals Directory on pages 165–172.

A NOTE ON USING CRYSTALS TOGETHER

When using more than one crystal at a time, it's important to choose stones that complement each other. Placing a crystal that calms you alongside a crystal that energizes you may result in the two of them cancelling each other out. You'll learn more about each crystal as you work through the pages of this book; use your intuition and your new crystal knowledge to create a crystal collection that truly supports you.

JANUARY

*There is nothing in the world more beautiful than the forest
clothed to its very hollows in snow. It is the still ecstasy of
nature, wherein every spray, every blade of grass, every
spire of reed, every intricacy of twig, is clad with radiance.*
– William Sharp

Following the winter solstice in December, January is a
time for reflection and planning for the forthcoming spring.
Named after the Roman god Janus, the protector of gates
who symbolized beginnings and endings, this month is one
of opportunity and of setting new paths to follow. It's a time
to start afresh with new resolutions and positive habits. This
month, take charge of your future and empower yourself to
fulfil your dreams, goals and intentions.

KEY DATES

WOLF MOON

The January full moon was named after hungry howling wolves during midwinter. This moon asks you to face your deepest feelings and fears with confidence. Carry **labradorite** (see opposite) to allay insecurities and spark empowerment during the moon's full phase.

1 JANUARY: NEW YEAR'S DAY

Set new intentions and goals for the year ahead. Visualize them coming into existence.

14 JANUARY: FESTIVAL OF *THORRABLÓT*

This Icelandic festival was originally celebrated in the old Norse month of Thorri and honours Thor, the god of thunder. Evoke the power of Thor by cutting out a thunderbolt shape and placing it on any object symbolic of a struggle you're facing (for example, place it on a textbook if you need help with your studies, or on an image of your current goal, such as a new home). Visualize the thunderbolt blasting any obstacles that stand in the way of you receiving what you desire.

LAST TUESDAY IN JANUARY: *UP HELLY AA*

A spectacular Shetland Viking fire festival celebrating the passing of Yule, and the fact that spring is in sight. Decorate your home with symbols of snow and fire, and ask the elements to bring you strength, protection and confidence for the seasons ahead.

JANUARY/FEBRUARY: LUNAR NEW YEAR

This celebration starts on the new moon and falls between 21 January and early February, lasting for around 16 days, until the full moon. This celebration ushers out the previous year and welcomes in the new, bringing with it opportunities, possibilities and luck. Famously celebrated in China, the Lunar New Year is also celebrated across much of East and South East Asia. Traditions include removing the bad and old, and welcoming the good and new. People may also worship their ancestors as part of this celebration, while businesses might make offerings to the gods of wealth and fortune.

CRYSTALS FOR JANUARY

While the nights are still at their darkest and the earth hibernates, these crystals will give you the support you crave.

CARNELIAN

Think warm, bold energy: a zing of joy that lifts your emotions like a ray of sunshine. Your confidence and endurance will build, helping you through the winter days and nights. This crystal is also wonderful for protecting your energy and bringing you bountiful good luck. Keep it close for a bubble of golden energy to keep you invigorated. Carnelian also stimulates tired muscles after a heavy workout, perfect for those new year trips to the gym – simply place it on the area that needs stimulation.

RED TIGER'S EYE

If you're feeling lethargic, this flashy crystal will lift your spirits while bringing a positive energy boost. Hold it close or wear it while you meditate for a deeper, more insightful meditation. Red tiger's eye is also beneficial for those of you wishing to take up a new health-focused hobby: it will ignite your passion and provide gentle self-love and encouragement.

ORANGE CALCITE

There are times when all we want is to feel lifted and joyful: this nurturing crystal is just the one to help you achieve this. It is the colour of sunshine, and has a zesty lightness that activates creativity. Connected to the sacral chakra, the seat of joy, it can help release anxiety and fear.

LABRADORITE

The crystal of transformation, labradorite is one of the most powerful protectors, shielding you from the negativity of the world. It helps remove fears and insecurities as you make significant life changes and plan for the future. Perfect when negotiating change.

CLEAR QUARTZ

This is a manifestation energy generator that will help you bring to fruition all that you desire. Keep it close when meditating or when visualizing the year ahead, and use that clear energy to create a supercharged crystal that will help you achieve anything you put your mind to. Said to be a master healer, it will also help keep those winter bugs at bay.

CITRINE

This crystal welcomes abundance in many forms. If you need a cash injection or an extra dose of luck at work, this crystal is one to keep close. Place it in the 'money corner' of your home – the furthest left corner from your front door, in a clutter-free space – and allow it to get to work.

MOONSTONE

When confronting new beginnings or setting in motion the wheels of change, the moonstone is a powerful crystal to have in your armoury. It helps to nurture your plans, giving them positivity and life, upping your chances of success.

ROSE QUARTZ

During periods of change, it is important to care for yourself. Rose quartz will give you a warm, gentle hug when you need it the most. As you forge new relationships, it will ensure they are healthy, respectful relationships, and that you are attracting the right people to work with you for your higher good.

FLUORITE

If your mind is racing with ideas and you're not sure where to start, fluorite will give you mental clarity and peace of mind. It also offers you the energy boost and motivation you need.

Top to bottom: moonstone (tumbles), fluorite (rough edge point), citrine (tumbles), clear quartz (point), orange calcite (sphere), labradorite (sphere), rose quartz (point), carnelian (pebble), red tiger's eye (tumbles)

NEW YEAR'S DAY RITUAL

Let your crystals bring your dreams to reality. It's time to welcome a bright new start and invite in the energy with which you hope to be surrounded over the coming year. Let's spark some thoughts and dreams and plant your manifestation seeds for the next 12 months.

1. Gather some paper, a pen and a crystal point – **citrine** and **clear quartz** are perfect for this (see page 14) – and find a comfortable space with no distractions.

2. List your intentions and dreams; be realistic about what you can achieve, but write with your desires and passions burning brightly. Let your internal fire spark your imagination.

3. Now visualize yourself living your best life. Hear the sounds in your imagination, feel the emotions and see the colours in your mind's eye. (This part of the exercise is a lovely time-out: repeat this any time you like to take a moment during the day to refocus.)

4. Place the paper under the crystal point and let the point face the sky and cosmos. Your intentions will radiate through the point out into the cosmos, and the universe will start aligning to help fulfil them.

5. Once you have received what you have asked for, either burn the list on the next full moon or give thanks and bury the list in the earth. Cleanse your crystal point using selenite, or charge it beneath the moonlight, ready to fulfil a fresh set of intentions (see page 176 for more on cleansing your crystals).

If you prefer, you can carry out this ritual visually, by cutting out pictures that represent your intentions and dreams to create a vision board.

THE OTTER

The inner child in each of us is represented by the otter. If you were born in January, or if you encounter the otter in a dream or as a significant symbol in your daily life, you are encouraged to not forget your sense of humour and true self.

The otter is also associated with exciting change being on the horizon. You are reminded not to dwell on the past, but instead to embrace new adventures and let the fun flow into your life. Don't worry; this doesn't mean forgetting important moments. If you have unresolved emotional conflict, call upon the otter to help you build bridges in relationships and family units, and create a larger support network. Otters are fierce protectors and represent independence and loyalty.

Use **rose quartz** (see page 14) or call upon the support of the otter while meditating to help you be more receptive to loving and playful energies while feeling a higher level of self-love and self-worth.

'I CAN AND I WILL'

As the year spans ahead, the notion of starting a new 12-month cycle can be daunting. Know that you already have everything within you that you need to make your wildest dreams happen, and take action when needed. If you are struggling to find motivation, stand in front of the mirror and tell yourself: 'I can and I will.'

For extra support, keep a **citrine** crystal close by (see page 14). Citrine is the merchant's crystal and will welcome success and abundance into your life. It also gives you a sense of joy and self-belief. Consider wearing it as a bracelet: it is said that wearing it on your left wrist will encourage the energy to flow towards you, while wearing it on your right will help the energy permeate through to your environment.

THE OTTER

PLANTS FOR JANUARY

Feature these plants in your altar, garden or floral displays to work their energies into your day, life, spells and intentions. Place a water-safe crystal in the soil next to your plants to encourage healthy growth and strong roots. **Clear quartz** (see page 14) is the perfect choice this month, as it will energize the soil and plant, helping to nourish the plant's energy.

CARNATION

Signifies love, fascination, distinction, protection, healing and strength.

SNOWDROP

Signifies purity, innocence and sympathy.

ROWAN TREE

Symbolizes courage, wisdom and protection.

SYMBOLIC ANIMAL FOR JANUARY

THE OX

The ox symbolizes hard work, positivity and honesty. To harness these properties, wear **red tiger's eye** or **fluorite** (see pages 13 and 14).

INTUITION RITUAL

The more we strengthen our intuition, the more clearly we receive its messages when making decisions, and the easier it becomes to trust our instincts.

1. Find a quiet space. Place a **clear quartz** crystal (see page 14) in your hand and have a notepad and pen close by.

2. Take five deep breaths. For each one, count to four as you breathe in, hold for two, then count to four as you breathe out.

3. Now place your hand on your heart and say out loud: 'Universe, I seek guidance. With every breath, I draw your wisdom closer. My question to you is this.' State your question, then continue: 'I feel safe in your presence, and open myself to receiving your divine message with gratitude and thanks.'

4. Open your eyes and write down whatever comes to mind, no matter how obscure. If you are not able to draw an answer, place the crystal by your bed for guidance as you dream.

FEBRUARY

To wandering children in the ages old,
I've often heard that mystic tales were told
Of fairy lands, where oft on trees and bowers
There fell from heaven pure crystal gems in showers.
Well, I believe, and so I think must you
That myths are shadows sometimes of the true;
For going forth upon a winter morn
A wondrous glory did the day adorn,
On every tree along the city street,
What matchless splendour did my vision greet.
Pendant from silver-coated branch and stem,
In argent beauty hung a brilliant gem;
Sparkling in candescent glory bright,
Shone myriad diamonds in the morning light.
Nature from its exhaustless wealth and store,
Through every street and by-way o'er and o'er,
Prodigal alike to all the rich and poor
Had scattered rivals to the koh-i-noor.
– 'February Gems', Allen R. Darrow

In February, we can see spring on the distant horizon.
Winter's magic starts to fade, while still just holding on to
the mystical darker nights and frosts. The name of the month
of love comes from the Latin word *februa*, which means
'to cleanse'. This is a month for reflecting and cleansing any
stagnation from your life. The month-long ancient Roman
festival Februalia traditionally saw the practice of purification
and atonement, with offerings and sacrifices made to
the gods.

KEY DATES

SNOW MOON

Named for the snowy weather that's common at this time of year, the February full moon signifies a renewal of spirit. It's time to reset and re-evaluate your soul's purpose. Are you really on your chosen path? **Clear quartz** (see page 26) will support you as you gain clarity of mind during the full moon and the following days.

JANUARY/FEBRUARY: LUNAR NEW YEAR (SEE PAGE 12)

This celebration starts on the new moon that falls between 21 January and early February, and lasts for around 16 days until the full moon.

1 FEBRUARY: IMBOLC OR ST BRIGID'S DAY

This pagan and traditional Gaelic festival is celebrated on the eve of 1 February, and is the second of the Sabbats celebrating the Earth's journey around the sun. Spring is in the air, and this festival celebrates light and fertility. Halfway between the depths of winter and the height of spring, it is the start of the farming year, when everything begins to grow and baby animals are born. Celebrations include washing away that which no longer serves you, welcoming in light and energy once again with the lighting of candles, and planting seeds. As you plant each seed, affirm a dream or goal; they will then grow along with the seeds. A great crystal to keep close by is **peach moonstone** (see page 28), for rebirth, new starts and transitions.

13–21 FEBRUARY: FESTIVAL OF PARENTALIA

A nine-day festival originally observed by the ancient Romans to honour their elders and ancestors and gain their wisdom, elements of this festival are now practised across many modern cultures. Take flowers to the graves of those who have passed and lay photos on your altar or display them elsewhere in your home. Encourage and welcome conversation about them with your family members and friends. Enjoy reminiscing and become imbued with wisdom from those past experiences.

14 FEBRUARY: ST VALENTINE'S DAY

Not just a day for romance, St Valentine's Day is the perfect day to show those you love how much you care. Send notes to your friends to show thanks for their support and guidance. Set a love spell by visualizing and listing the attributes you want in a partner, then place under a piece of **clear** or **rose quartz** (see page 26) to amplify the energy.

15 FEBRUARY: LUPERCALIA

This pagan festival is considered by some to be the origin of St Valentine's Day. A festival of purification, to banish evil spirits, ward off negative energy, and welcome loving and abundant energies, Lupercalia was first celebrated in Ancient Rome. Call upon the Roman and pagan deity Lupa (the goddess of rural life, fertility of the fields and the harvest) to help you as you clear any bad vibes from your life using **black tourmaline** (see page 28), smudge smoke or incense smoke. Place the crystal by your front door or wear it for personal protection. Light the smudge or incense and direct it into every corner of every room, including the cupboards. A popular way to do this is by using a feather or fan. Then open all the windows to allow the energy to escape.

CRYSTALS FOR FEBRUARY

As the nights start to lighten and the earth begins to wake, these crystals will give you the support you crave.

AMETHYST

Being so closely linked to Aquarians, this incredible crystal is a must for February. A powerful mood stabilizer, amethyst will bring emotional stability as you connect with the awakening energy of the earth. It helps strengthen relationships and will bring courage as you embark on new paths, as well as keeping any doubts, anxiety and stresses at bay during your day-to-day life.

RED GARNET

Perfect for the root chakra (at the base of the spine), this wholesome gemstone will keep you grounded and your energy rooted. It is one of the oldest spiritual protectors, ideal for when you are practising rituals and calling on ancestral wisdom. A crystal of prosperity, gratitude and abundance, keep this close by to welcome in a plethora of positive changes. This gem is said to keep your metabolism working to the best of its ability; carry a piece with you to help support your metabolic health.

ROSE QUARTZ

As well as being a crystal of love – perfect for February – this beautiful pink stone is linked to the heart chakra, and is like a wonderful warm hug when you need it the most. It supports you through emotional changes and inspires compassion, within you and within those around you. Use it to attract relationships with truth and meaning.

CLEAR QUARTZ

Use this crystal's clear energy during February alongside another crystal, to boost its energy; this will allow you to amplify the properties of the crystal you have paired it with.

Top to bottom: rose quartz (point), red garnet (freeform), rhodonite (rough point), clear quartz (point), yellow jasper (tumble), amethyst (cluster), peach moonstone (pebble), black tourmaline (raw)

PEACH MOONSTONE

Keep a piece close to boost fertility and reproductive health in the month of love. Peach moonstone is also great for new starts and bringing luck with business opportunities, making it an empowering crystal to wear.

BLACK TOURMALINE

A talisman of protection and purification, this crystal is a powerful spiritual weapon. Imagine a forcefield surrounding you, repelling any negative vibes that may be trying to bring you down; that is what this incredible crystal can do for you in the final month of winter.

YELLOW JASPER

As the dark starts making way for lighter mornings and nights, this beautiful stone brings a ray of sunshine, boosting your confidence and inner strength. It is protective during spiritual work and helps you facilitate good communication with your guides. It also allows you to welcome wisdom, happiness and joy as we head towards the first signs of spring.

RHODONITE

Where **rose quartz** welcomes love and friendship, rhodonite enhances love, letting it run deeper and more passionately. This pink wonder is also beneficial to have around to help soothe emotional upset and trauma. It is well known to be supportive during times of heartbreak, empowering you to heal in a nurturing, healthy way.

CARNELIAN

This beautiful, zingy stone will give you the energy boost you need during the dark nights of February. Carnelian will help you to build your confidence: use this stone to motivate you and become a stronger version of yourself.

RED TIGER'S EYE

Red tiger's eye is the perfect stone to ignite your passions and give you an energy boost. Hold it close to alleviate your fears and worries, and to find the encouragement you need to build strength. Especially useful for meditation, this crystal also provides insight and motivation.

PLANTS FOR FEBRUARY

Feature these in your altar, garden or floral displays to work their energies into your day, life, spells and intentions. **Amethyst** (see page 26) is water-safe, making it an ideal crystal for you to place directly in the soil for plant purity and health this month.

VIOLET

Symbolizes innocence, modesty, everlasting love, truth and loyalty.

PRIMROSE

Symbolizes a deep-running love, the emotions of first love, and youth and renewal.

BEECH TREE

The rise of new beginnings, prosperity, new experiences and challenges.

SYMBOLIC ANIMAL FOR FEBRUARY

THE TIGER

The tiger symbolizes strength and fearlessness. To harness these properties, wear **carnelian** or **red tiger's eye** (see page 28).

LOVE BLOCK CLEANSING RITUAL

Carry out this ritual during the month of love to support cleansing and atonement within your relationships.

1. Gather a piece of soap or some bodywash, a candle and a piece of food grown from the earth (see below).

2. Start by showering or taking a bath. Begin to think of barriers that are hindering you from finding love and building lasting relationships. It's also important to take this time to consider anything you wish to make amends for, in preparation for turning over a new leaf in your relationships.

3. Visualize the soap scrubbing away these barriers; watch as any associated negative energy is rinsed down the plughole. Feel empowered as you let them go; notice the positive energy wash over and energize you.

4. Light your chosen candle to invoke the element of fire into your ritual and to welcome the energy associated with the candle colour into your life.

5. Eat your chosen fruit, vegetable, seeds or nuts to welcome the earth element.

6. Now that you are imbued with loving energy, think about exactly what you desire. Write it down and visualize receiving it, giving thanks in advance.

*If you're looking for your special someone, write a comprehensive list of the qualities of the person you would like to welcome into your life, in as much detail as possible. Place under a **rose quartz** point (see page 26, or turn to page 175 for more on crystal shapes).*

SOAP OR BODY WASH

Choose lemon, orange, sage or eucalyptus for an invigorating cleanse.

CANDLE

Choose yellow for friendships, pink for romance, green for luck, black for protection, blue for peace, white for purification and red for passion.

FOOD

Choose carrots, figs, pomegranates or apples, all of which will give you a burst of loving energy. Alternatively, choose seeds and nuts.

THE SEAHORSE

Seahorses symbolize helpfulness. They teach us to help those in need when they need it the most. The seahorse's spirit teaches us what it means to give without expecting.

This beautiful creature and February babies both bring the gift of peace and patience to your life. They are magical and unique, and able to connect with anyone they come across. These are especially nurturing beings.

If you encounter the seahorse in your dreams, or as a prevalent symbol in your daily life, you are being told to take heed, pause and gain perspective on your current situation. The seahorse's energy will support you to venture through any obstacles you may have come across with ease.

If you feel connected with the seahorse, you are driven to help others, but you must listen to your instinct and practise self-care to diffuse any emotional energy you may have absorbed. When you are called to help, you will therefore be grounded, with the waves around you steady.

AFFIRMATION FOR FEBRUARY

'ALL THAT I NEED IS WITHIN ME'

As you embrace the loving February energy, take the time to practise loving yourself a little bit more. Look at how much you have achieved up until this very moment and take a second to feel proud of yourself. This month, do not feel guilty for taking time for yourself. Embrace the hobbies you love and be reassured that time you enjoy wasting is not wasted time at all. Remember, too, that your best days still haven't happened yet.

You are a beautiful soul who is loved and important, even to people you haven't yet met. Carry a **rose quartz** or **rhodonite** crystal (see pages 26 and 28) with you to foster loving energy, and to encourage other people to behave more lovingly towards you too.

THE SEAHORSE

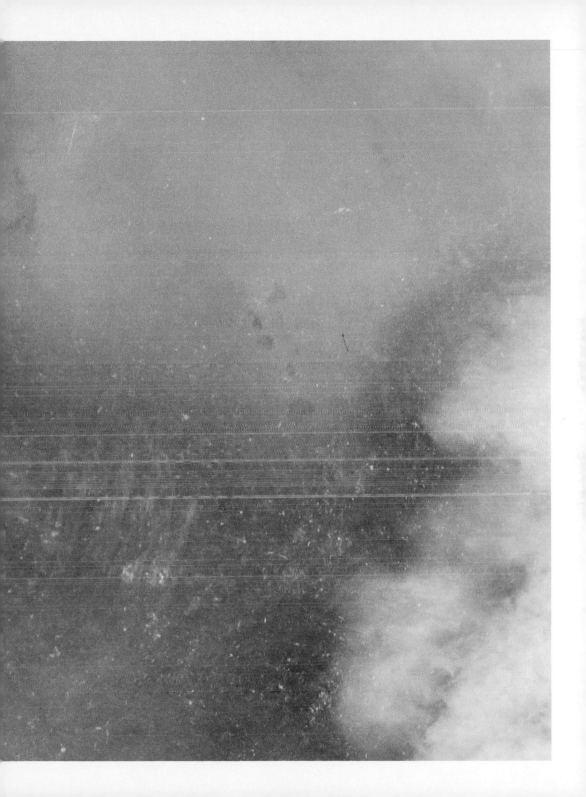

SPRING

SPRING STARTS WITH THE SPRING EQUINOX
ON AROUND 20 MARCH AND INCLUDES
THE MONTHS OF MARCH, APRIL AND MAY,
BEFORE HANDING OVER TO SUMMER AT THE
SUMMER SOLSTICE ON AROUND 20 JUNE.
AS THE WEATHER STARTS TO WARM, NATURE
SPRINGS TO LIFE AND COLOUR RETURNS
TO NATURE.

A time of new starts, birth and hope, spring encourages you: embrace the day, try that new hobby, make amends. Use the energy growing from the ground to empower you as you embark upon a new path, and turn it into confidence, if you need a little extra. The sun is starting to shine and warm the flowers, and their colours and scents are the perfect inspiration for getting creative. Feel the joy present in this season.

At the spring equinox, the sun is directly above the equator. This is scientifically significant, but an equinox also brings so much to our lives spiritually due to the symbolism of darkness and light. This equinox is a beacon of hope and light; it celebrates the fact that the days are now longer than the nights. Brighter days are coming, and are paving the way for us to fulfil our ambitions. Life is awakening and the possibilities are endless. Seize all opportunities with both hands, and embrace the sun's energy to help you pursue your hopes and dreams – above and beyond what you have wished for.

SPRING ZODIAC SIGNS

PISCES
(19 FEBRUARY–20 MARCH)

Element: Water
Birthstone: Aquamarine – keep this close by for emotional clarity
Lucky crystals: Yellow jasper and yellow sapphire
Soulmates: Cancer and Scorpio
Ruling planets: Jupiter and Neptune
Lucky numbers: 3 and 7
Lucky days: Tuesday, Thursday and Sunday
Colours: Turquoise, green and aqua

ARIES
(21 MARCH– 20 APRIL)

Element: Fire
Birthstone: Diamond – keep this close by for inner strength
Lucky crystals: Amethyst and red jasper
Soulmates: Leo and Sagittarius
Ruling planet: Mars
Lucky numbers: 6 and 9
Lucky days: Tuesday, Friday and Saturday
Colours: Red and scarlet

TAURUS
(21 APRIL–20 MAY)

Element: Earth
Birthstone: Emerald – keep this close by for success and love
Lucky crystals: Quartz, coral and emerald
Soulmates: Virgo and Capricorn
Ruling planet: Venus
Lucky numbers: 5 and 6
Lucky days: Monday, Friday and Saturday
Colours: White and green

GEMINI
(21 MAY–20 JUNE)

Element: Air
Birthstone: Moonstone – keep this close by for positivity and balance
Lucky crystals: Aquamarine and agate
Soulmates: Libra and Aquarius
Ruling planet: Mercury
Lucky numbers: 5, 6, 14, 23 and 32
Lucky days: Monday, Wednesday and Thursday
Colours: Green, yellow and orange

MARCH

Never mind, March, we know
When you blow
You're not really mad
Or angry or bad;
You're only blowing the winter away
To get the world ready for April and May.
– 'Never Mind, March', Annette Wynne

March is the month where the cold still staves off the arriving warmth, and the last of the snow hasn't quite left us yet. The frost paints the nights and the sun warms the days. Spring is arriving, and the dark is making way for light as we celebrate the rebirth of nature, the awakening of the sun, the spring equinox and new life.

March was the first calendar month in the Roman calendar and was named for the Roman god of war, Mars. With this in mind, it can be said to symbolize new beginnings, so now is the perfect time for making new goals, attacking projects, planning adventures and welcoming in new opportunities. It is not the time to stand still.

KEY DATES

WORM MOON

This full moon is said to have been named the Worm Moon for at this time the worms would start venturing over the newly thawed ground, leaving trails behind them. During this full moon, look at your inner self more closely. What do you crave? More knowledge, self-care, exercise? Take this opportunity to set the wheels in motion and make it happen. Keep **iolite** (see opposite) close by to regain motivation and balance in life.

MID-MARCH: HOLI FESTIVAL OF COLOUR

This Hindu festival celebrates the arrival of spring. It symbolizes the triumph of good over evil and is celebrated by people throwing coloured powders over each other at specially organized parties.

17 MARCH: ST PATRICK'S DAY

A joyous occasion of parties, dancing and singing, held on the date of the death of St Patrick, the patron saint of Ireland. This is a wonderful day for letting go and banishing any negatives from your life. Wear green and gold to welcome success and luck as spring gets underway.

20–21 MARCH: THE SPRING EQUINOX – OSTARA

This is the third of the Sabbats celebrating the Earth's journey around the sun, the pagan celebration of the first day of spring, as the day and night are now of equal lengths and in perfect balance. Ostara was named after the goddess Eostra, encouraging you to take stock of your life and bring things into balance. If you have been working too much or not practising enough self-care, now is the time to address this.

CRYSTALS FOR MARCH

As you start a new season and a quest for life balance, use the following crystals to help you on your way.

AQUAMARINE

This beautiful, sea-coloured crystal will empower you to let go of that which no longer serves you, and to trust in the power of new beginnings. It offers protection and brings you luck through the new season – and all its new adventures. Rest a piece of aquamarine on your throat if you are scheduled to make a speech, as it will help to fine tune your communication skills.

BLOODSTONE

If you're looking to take a more creative approach in life, this is the crystal for you. Offering you protection and guidance as you stride forwards, it will also heighten your intuition as you choose which direction to go in, or what to cut from your life to help you find that much-needed balance. As you ramp up your activity levels in spring, you may find yourself drinking more water; if you suffer with bladder complaints, this stone is said to offer support.

IOLITE

Containing the energy of twilight within, iolite is known as the Viking's compass. It is the perfect stone to awaken your dreams, enhance your intuition and usher in the confidence you need to explore your opportunities. It helps you to recover balance, physically, emotionally and spiritually, and restores a sense of perspective.

TURQUOISE

Although often associated with December, this beautiful stone also works well with March's energy to bring luck, serenity, peace and protection. Keep it close by as a day-to-day talisman to support you in your endeavours.

SELENITE

Think calm, purity, serenity and peace: these words embody selenite. Yet this energy-generating crystal is also one of the most powerful crystals, thanks to its ability to cleanse and charge other stones. If your home environment is stressful, place selenite in any room where you crave calm to lower its vibrations to a gentle simmer.

RAINBOW MOONSTONE

If it's time to awaken your intuition and tune into your clairvoyance, then this flashy gem will be your muse. When used during meditation, it has the ability to awaken your crown and third-eye chakras, improving your spiritual clarity as you seek answers.

TIGER'S EYE

During change and especially during times of upheaval, it is important to stay balanced, stable and grounded so as not to run away with opportunities not meant for us. Tiger's eye will level you and reconnect you with the earth – plus it will attract wealth and prosperity for good measure.

CLEAR QUARTZ

Clear quartz is the perfect crystal for visualizing your future hopes and dreams, and manifesting them into existence. Use this stone when meditating or during the ritual on page 44 – it will attract positive thoughts and gratitude as you ask the universe for what you wish to receive.

BLACK TOURMALINE

The perfect problem-solving stone, black tourmaline can be used both to find logical solutions to issues you may be having, and to protect you from negativity. Use it to banish problems, pests and negative energy to keep your outlook positive for spring.

Left to right: aquamarine (tumbles), selenite (pebble), bloodstone (elephant), iolite (freeform), rainbow moonstone (point), tiger's eye (tumbles)

NEW BEGINNINGS RITUAL

This ritual is most powerful when used on the spring equinox. However, you can adapt it whenever you wish to manifest an intention or goal and use it as needed.

1. Gather a piece of paper, a pen and a **clear quartz** crystal (see page 42).

2. Start by closing your eyes, then breathe in and out, and feel your feet planted firmly on the ground.

3. Open your eyes. Write down everything you'd like to receive or achieve during the spring and before the summer solstice.

4. Place the list beneath the crystal: this will amplify the words and energy of your intentions.

5. Place your hand on the crystal and visualize your desired events happening. Picture them in bright colour.

6. Give thanks to the crystal and the universe, and recite the following verse to let the universe know you are ready to receive:

   As the dark turns to day,
   As the sun lights the way,
   As the Earth awakes,
   As new beginnings bake,
   Let my words and dreams grow to reality,
   For I am worthy of the aspirations I make,
   I am grateful for all I am about to receive,
   Let the abundance of light flow to me.

7. Leave the paper in a place where you will see it often. Every time you look at it, visualize your new beginnings happening clearly in your mind's eye.

8. Once you receive what you have asked for, give thanks to the sun and return the paper to the earth by burying it.

MARCH'S ANIMAL PERSONALITY

THE DEER

The deer is a symbol of calm, serenity and compassion. If the deer visits you in your dreams, or if you encounter a deer in nature, it may be a sign that your life needs more peace. You may also be feeling troubled and unbalanced in your friendships, especially if you are giving them lots of physical and mental energy. Those born in March tend to enjoy being surrounded by like-minded people. Call upon the deer – either out loud or in your thoughts – to help you find aligned, like-minded souls, whose presence will nurture your existence rather than drain it.

The deer is also an animal of grace and will encourage you to listen more closely to your intuition. Trust in your abilities and you'll be shown the path to success. Allow the deer to light your path and give you strength through difficult times.

THE RABBIT

The rabbit symbolizes sensitivity and new beginnings. To harness these properties, wear **selenite** and **rainbow moonstone** (see page 42).

PLANTS FOR MARCH

Feature these in your altar, garden or floral displays to work their energies into your day, life, spells and intentions. If you are having trouble with pests on your plants this month, place **black tourmaline** (see page 42) at the base to repel them.

DAFFODIL

Symbolizes hope and renewal.

HONEYSUCKLE

Symbolizes good luck, good fortune and protection from evil.

MAGNOLIA TREE

Symbolizes purity, nobility and healing.

AFFIRMATION FOR MARCH

'I WELCOME CALM AND BALANCE INTO MY LIFE'

March is an exciting time for many, and it is very normal to literally feel like you have a spring in your step around the time of the spring equinox. Let this energy invigorate you, but hold off making any big decisions until you feel the balance has been restored. Practise saying, 'I welcome calm and balance into my life,' to keep yourself grounded, and carry **selenite** (see page 42) with you for a dose of calming energy if you feel overwhelmed and want to be brought back to earth.

APRIL

There is no time like Spring,
When life's alive in everything,
Before new nestlings sing,
Before cleft swallows speed their journey back
Along the trackless track,
God guides their wing,
He spreads their table that they nothing lack,
Before the daisy grows a common flower,
Before the sun has power
To scorch the world up in his noontime hour.
– 'Spring', Christina Rossetti

As nature begins to flourish and new life starts to appear, April prepares us for brighter days ahead. The spring sunshine sets in, energizing us to cleanse our lives and homes of stale energies. This is where the term 'spring cleaning' comes from. In fact, the term is associated with the Persian New Year, which falls on the first day of spring. Iranians continue the practice of *khaneh tekani* today. It literally translates as 'shaking the house', and everything in the home is thoroughly cleansed, from the curtains to the carpets. It's also traditional to buy new clothes to wear for the new year and to purchase flowers, such as hyacinths and tulips. The word April is of Latin origin, meaning 'opening', which makes it the perfect time to embrace opportunities.

KEY DATES

PINK MOON

Named after the early blooming wildflower phlox, this is a full moon for newness, freshness and for letting go of things that no longer serve you. It's a time for change and growth. Use **rose quartz** (see page 52) for strength when letting go of deeply rooted emotions.

22 APRIL: EARTH DAY

A day to celebrate our beautiful Earth, and to celebrate the achievements of those making a difference to saving it. On this day – and all year round, if you can – take part in activities to clean up your local area, and swap out a product that you frequently use for another, more environmentally friendly alternative. You could do something as simple as turning off the lights when you're not in a room; small changes make a huge difference.

23 APRIL: ST GEORGE'S DAY

A celebration of the noble Christian saint, but also a day to celebrate our own strengths and be proud of our achievements. Look back to see how far you have come, and consider past adversities you have faced and overcome. On this day, it's a popular tradition to purchase or gift a **clear quartz** (see opposite) for clarity and empowerment through the rest of the year.

30 APRIL–1 MAY: WALPURGISNACHT

This is a traditional German and Norse celebration when witches have fun. They exchange gifts such as crystals and books, eat food decorated with sigils and pentagrams, and practise fun and uplifting witchcraft.

CRYSTALS FOR APRIL

As you cleanse away old energies and welcome in the new, I recommend the following crystals to help you on your way.

CARNELIAN

The colour of deep rays emanating from the sun, this beautiful crystal stimulates joy and motivation. It's perfect for an extra boost of energy when spring cleaning, starting new projects and beginning to venture out into the world again after the colder months of hibernation. If your muscles grow tired when organizing your home or cleaning, carnelian will help them recover.

CLEAR QUARTZ

This exquisite crystal will boost your spiritual and emotional energy, clearing the mind, body and spirit of clutter and aligning your crown chakra. Get ready for the spring zing! As a master healer, this crystal will support you with any ailment that you direct it to and ask for support with.

FLUORITE

A spiritual detoxification crystal, this incredible gem neutralizes negative energies. Simply being in the same room as this crystal can raise your vibrations and enhance your natural aura. Fluorite is also said to ease cold symptoms: keep one in your pocket or wear on a bracelet to feel the benefits if you suffer from hayfever. As an added bonus, it can also help with anxiety.

PREHNITE

If you are an empath, a teacher, a carer or if you work in the medical profession, you will often find yourself surrounded by heightened human emotions. This can deplete your own energy, leaving you feeling overwhelmed, sad and heavy. Prehnite, and **prehnite with epidote**, will unburden you of emotional attachments and allow you to care for others without taking on their worries as your own. This makes it the ideal crystal for giving yourself a spring clean.

SUNSTONE

We can always welcome more abundance into our lives, and this stone brings joy in waves. Perfect for April thanks to its ability to inspire good-natured enjoyment of life, along with energy and leadership, sunstone is ideal for helping you to organize your life and home.

LAPIS LAZULI

The stone of truth and friendship, lapis lazuli is wonderful to have around when spring cleaning your relationships. It is important to be aware of those energies that can cause upset, and drain rather than uplift you. You will feel empowered to talk to your loved ones in a gentle but productive way. Lapis lazuli also attunes you to the feelings of others, so it is great for deepening relationships.

LABRADORITE

The perfect crystal companion during periods of transformation, labradorite will build your strength, bolster your intuition and protect you against negativity. This beautiful stone helps you to set your intentions and persevere when following them through.

ROSE QUARTZ

Full of loving energy, rose quartz will attract love and friendship to you, while also supporting you to practise self-care and show yourself the kindness you deserve. Use it to build your self-confidence and respect for yourself, and to inject a healthy dose of passion into your life.

ONYX

Associated with the root chakra, this powerfully protective crystal will keep you grounded while helping you to build power, stamina and self-control. Use onyx to support you during times of grief or intense stress. This stone also imparts wisdom, beneficial for decision-making.

Top to bottom: lapiz lazuli (point), sunstone (point), clear quartz (point), carnelian (pebble), fluorite (rough edge point), phrehnite (point)

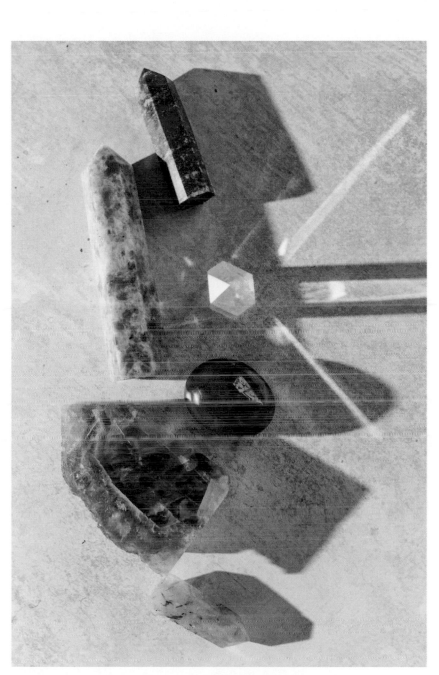

SPRING CLEANING RITUAL

Carry out this ritual on a sunny day for an extra dose of motivation.

1. Gather natural cleaning supplies, especially any products with citrus scents for an invigorating and fresh clean.

2. First, declutter. As you pick up each item, ask yourself if it benefits you emotionally or spiritually, or if it will help as you work towards your future goals. There's no need to part with items of real sentimental value, but if you're still holding a magazine from last month that now displays cup rings and takeaway stains, you know what to do.

3. After an honest declutter, it's important to start cleaning from the top of the house, quite literally. De-cobweb the upstairs rooms first, then use your citrus-scented products to wipe the surfaces and skirting boards. Lastly, vacuum. Cleaning in this order will help you capture and banish old settled energies, while ensuring they don't resettle on already cleansed areas.

4. Open the windows of your home and say out loud: 'Energies of old and past, we invite you to leave our home as your work here is done. New energy, we welcome you in to bring light, joy and abundant energies, for now and the future.'

5. To rid yourself of old energies, both physically and symbolically, dispose of your cleaning cloths once you have finished.

SYMBOLIC ANIMAL FOR APRIL

THE HAWK

The hawk symbolizes self-confidence and passion. To harness these properties, wear **sunstone** or **rose quartz** (see page 52).

PLANTS FOR APRIL

Feature these in your altar, garden or floral displays to work their energies into your day, life, spells and intentions. **Onyx** will help your fruits - especially tomato plants – to grow in an abundant and healthy way this month.

FORGET-ME-NOT

Symbolizes true love and faithfulness.

HYACINTH

Symbolizes peace, commitment and beauty.

TULIP

Symbolizes perfect deep love.

CHERRY BLOSSOM TREE

Symbolizes a time for renewal and new life.

AFFIRMATION FOR APRIL

'CHANGE IS NOT JUST PART OF LIFE. CHANGE IS LIFE. LIFE IS CHANGE.'

As you cleanse the old from your life and make way for the new, this is the perfect time for reflection. What no longer serves you? What no longer brings you joy? What would you like to spend more time doing?

Keep **labradorite** (see page 52) close by as you repeat this affirmation to bolster your intuition as you make decisions. It will also guide you during times of change and transformation.

APRIL'S ANIMAL PERSONALITY

THE CHEETAH

If the cheetah visits you in your dreams or appears as a significant symbol in your day-to-day life, it could be a sign that you need to regain focus. It's time to seize the day if you want to reap the rewards of the seeds you have sown over the past 12 months. Go and grab exactly what you want; keep your eyes on the prize and your dreams will be yours.

If you were born in April, the cheetah reminds you that it's OK to let go of your emotions and release them through crying. In fact, it's important to do this to stay emotionally healthy. It's not a sign of weakness; you must release the energy from others' emotions that you have absorbed. Going forwards, keep a **prehnite with epidote** crystal (see page 51) close by; this will guard you against others' emotions and will stop you carrying them home.

MAY

If I could stay up late no doubt
I'd catch the buds just bursting out;
And up from every hidden root
Would jump a tiny slender shoot;
I wonder how seeds learn the way,
They always know the very day –
The pretty, happy first of May;
If I could stay up then, no doubt
I'd catch the buds just bursting out.
– 'The First of May', Annette Wynne

May is named after the Greek goddess Maia, identified as the goddess of the growth of plants, perfect for the final month of spring. There is an emphasis on mental strength and security in alignment with the zodiac signs Taurus and Gemini, so it's the perfect time to work on new projects and move towards abundance. It is a fruitful month, so use this time to sow seeds and use the fertility connection to grow your own powers if you wish; it's also an ideal time for those starting or growing a family.

KEY DATES

FLOWER MOON

As the spring flowers come to life, this full moon celebrates the start of the summer flowering gardens. The Flower Moon encourages you to express your creativity and be open with your ideas. The standard gold **tiger's eye** (see opposite) will unlock your creative juices, so carry a piece whenever you are planning to work on a project that requires your full attention. It will bring you luck and usher in good fortune.

1 MAY: BELTANE – MAY DAY

The fourth of the Sabbats celebrating the Earth's journey around the sun, this is a popular pagan holiday. Celebrated roughly between Ostara (the spring equinox) and Lithia (the summer solstice), it is also popularly known as May Day. It is celebrated with bonfires, maypoles, dancing and the performance of fertility rituals. Many people wear flowers or weave them into their hair in a beautiful celebration of spring. It's a popular time to try to conceive; surround your bed with **moonstone** crystals (see opposite), flowers and green leaves for an extra dose of fertility magic.

4 MAY: FESTIVAL OF *SHEELA–NA–GIG*

Another celebration of fertility – in fact, May in its entirety is considered to be a fertile month. You only have to look around in nature to see the new baby animals and the budding plants, bulbs and trees to see why. This particular festival is for celebrating the mother figures in your life, both biological and non-biological: all those who give you life, security and guidance.

CRYSTALS FOR MAY

These crystals will support you on your quest to create a more fertile environment or birth new projects.

MOONSTONE

The crystal of new starts and fertility, this joyous gem will nurture and support you as you embark on life-changing adventures. Keep a piece in your pocket or under your pillow for new ideas or fertile energy whenever you need it. If you are feeling stressed, team up moonstone with a **rose quartz** for fertility, or **amethyst** for new projects.

EMERALD

This crystal will bestow love and successful new relationships, promoting compassion, unity and balance in partnerships both romantic and platonic. It will also instil intuition and give you clear sight when making big decisions for your future. It is said to soothe the eyes and sinuses; if you feel an attack of hayfever coming on, place a piece on your heart chakra and lie down, imagining the green energy flowing to your eyes and forehead. Alternatively, place a piece directly on your forehead.

RED JASPER

Long considered a stone for increased fertility, this is a crystal to keep under your mattress. Alternatively, carry it in a pocket close to your sacral chakra – below your naval and above the base of your spine. Not only will it work with the chakra, it will ground and root your emotions, reducing your stress levels.

TIGER'S EYE

Though it's considered a fun, lucky stone that brings good fortune, tiger's eye also has a serious side. It helps you to redirect any excess energy that may be creating distractions into areas of your life that need it more. This makes it ideal for when you're setting your sights on new projects.

CITRINE

Especially suitable for fun-loving and sociable May Geminis, citrine promotes abundance and brings you luck in any projects started during this time. It will attract success and help drive you on to the right path. If you feel a pull in a new direction, it could well be citrine illuminating your life's path.

MOSS AGATE

Any practical problems you come up against can be resolved quickly with moss agate in your corner; in fact, any **agate** is beneficial when it comes to finding answers. It is especially helpful at times of introspection, such as when identifying problems that need resolving, or events you need to move on from.

PINK TOURMALINE

If you are suffering from stress and anxiety, pink tourmaline will calm your emotions and soothe your mental health, taking you to a place where you can make sense of the situation. This will empower you to take control and take measured steps towards a healthy resolution.

LAPIS LAZULI

This beautiful gold-flecked crystal is known as the stone of truth and friendship. Use it to encourage harmony and wisdom, and to foster meaningful relationships with others.

FLUORITE

Fluorite brings energy, motivation and mental clarity – use it to focus a racing mind and to sharpen your intellect. This is also useful as a spiritual detoxification crystal, perfect for neutralizing negative energy.

SMOKY QUARTZ

Perfect for use in times of stress, smoky quartz neutralizes negative vibrations and helps you to relax. Keep it close to alleviate your fears, ease any pressure you may feel mounting up, and to help eliminate feelings of guilt.

Left to right: pink tourmaline (pebble) red jasper (raw), emerald (rough), moss agate (point), citrine (point), grey agate (tumble), moonstone (tumbles), tiger's eye (tumbles)

BELTANE RITUALS

There are many rituals and traditions conducted in May. Here are a few simple yet powerful rituals you can practise with ease.

RIBBONS RITUAL

Write wishes, acknowledgements of gratitude and blessings on ribbons and tie them to a tree.

GARDEN RITUAL

Create a space in your garden for new plants, herbs or flowers. Include a piece of standing stone in the centre of the space: not only will this connect you to your ancestors, but it will also draw the sun to this area of the garden and create a protective force. You can make this a feature of your whole garden, if you wish, by arranging plants and flowers around the standing stone.

FERTILITY FOOD RITUAL

Eat fruit pastries, chocolates, almonds, asparagus, pineapples, strawberries, oysters and vanilla in abundance to act as aphrodisiacs and to welcome spring fortune and fertility.

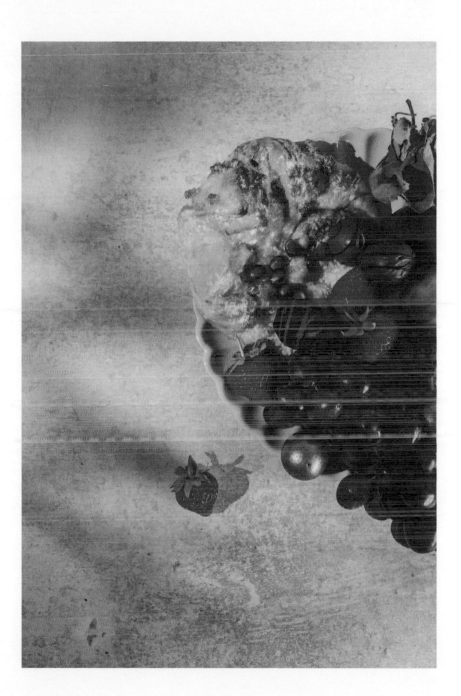

NEW MOON FERTILITY RITUAL

Practise this ritual on the May new moon.

1. Gather lavender essential oil, olive oil, a pair of gloves, a green candle, white paper, a green pen, dried pine needles, matches and a fireproof bowl.

2. Mix together two drops of lavender oil and two drops of olive oil. Ensure you wear gloves to protect your skin from the strong essential oil, then rub the mixture on to the candle.

3. Write your fertility wishes on the paper using the green pen, then scatter over a few dried pine needles. Fold the paper with the pine needles inside.

4. Light the candle and say: 'Child of mine, with love and protection, we welcome you to our lives. Your (father/mother) and I await to bless you with love and wisdom; share this abundant and happy life with us. We are waiting for you.'

5. Hold the paper over the candle flame until it catches fire, then place the paper in the fireproof bowl to burn out.

6. Allow the candle to burn out completely; don't leave it unattended at any time.

7. Once both are extinguished, bury the remains under your bedroom window, or in a plant pot on your windowsill if this isn't possible.

8. As and when your spell manifests, give thanks to the new moon.

PLANTS FOR MAY

Feature these in your altar, garden or floral displays to work their energies into your day, life, spells and intentions. **Jasper** of any colour (see page 61) will encourage new growth, so if you have given a plant a bit of an overenthusiastic trim, it will spread its branches again before you know it.

GERANIUM

Symbolizes true happiness, good health, good wishes and friendship.

AQUILEGIA

Symbolizes endurance, faith and peace.

HAWTHORNE TREE

Symbolizes love and protection.

SYMBOLIC ANIMAL FOR MAY

THE TURTLE

The turtle symbolizes wisdom and intelligence. To harness these properties, use **lapis lazuli** for wisdom or **fluorite** for intelligence (see page 62).

MAY'S ANIMAL PERSONALITY

THE FOX

If the fox visits you in your dreams or you encounter it in your day-to-day life, it is a sign that you need to think on your feet and take quick action. The solution to a problem is right in front of your eyes; you just need to seize the day. The fox is a reminder to stay on the straight and narrow, though, and to avoid taking the easy route out if it leads to corruption. While the fox does symbolize trickery and slyness, it is often misunderstood. The fox is a calculated risk-taker and can be successful at anything it puts its mind to – so long as it stays on the right path. Use creativity, intelligence and flexibility when facing dilemmas, and embrace your own psychic gifts to awaken your intuition.

If you were born in May, it is said that, like the fox, you are highly protective of your own space. Self-motivated and strong-willed, you work hard to fulfil your goals, usually with great success. You love to receive affection, and you crave attention and reassurance. Take confidence in your abilities: you are capable of anything.

AFFIRMATION FOR MAY

'I SHOW MYSELF THE SAME FORGIVENESS I OFFER MY LOVED ONES'

Be kind to yourself as you navigate your way through the tests and tribulations you face. It is imperative that you forgive yourself and accept that you cannot be blamed for things beyond your control. Be kind to yourself, find inner peace and allow yourself to be at one with the past as you move towards an exciting future of endless possibilities.

Keep **smoky quartz** (see page 62) close by to eliminate feelings of guilt and to ease pressure. **Pink tourmaline** (see page 62) will help you find feelings of peace and self-forgiveness as you move forwards into a new chapter.

THE FOX

SUMMER

TRADITIONALLY THE WARMEST SEASON OF
THE YEAR, SUMMER STARTS AT THE SUMMER
SOLSTICE ON AROUND 20 JUNE AND LASTS
UNTIL THE AUTUMN EQUINOX ON AROUND
20 SEPTEMBER.

As the summer sun heats up, vitality and energy will surround you in
abundance. Fun is at your fingertips, so why not plan that party or
get-together? Make amends and heal old wounds while you take action
in your life. Use this time wisely and move forwards with your ideas, as it's
a time when opportunities will come to fruition. Think carefully about any
surprise offers; they may not be what they seem.

The summer solstice marks the longest day of the year and occurs when the
sun is directly above the the Tropic of Cancer. This solstice welcomes light, and
celebrates the triumph of light over darkness. Draw on this energy to celebrate
the light within you and use it to empower yourself in all that you do. It's a time
for joy and relaxation. Take time to connect with the sun by being in nature;
watch the sunset and feel the rays on your face. As you do so, visualize what
you'd like to receive or achieve and feel the energy radiating from the sun,
ready to make this happen.

SUMMER ZODIAC SIGNS

GEMINI
(21 MAY–20 JUNE)

Element: Earth
Birthstone: Moonstone – keep this close by for positivity and balance
Lucky crystals: Aquamarine and agate
Soulmates: Libra and Aquarius
Ruling planet: Mercury
Lucky numbers: 5, 6, 14, 23 and 32
Lucky days: Monday, Wednesday and Thursday
Colours: Green, yellow and orange

CANCER
(21 JUNE–22 JULY)

Element: Water
Birthstone: Ruby – keep this close by for harmony and calm
Lucky crystals: Moonstone and pearl
Soulmates: Scorpio and Pisces
Ruling planet: Moon
Lucky numbers: 2, 7 and 9
Lucky days: Tuesday, Thursday, Friday and Sunday
Colours: Blue and silver

LEO
(23 JULY–22 AUGUST)

Element: Fire
Birthstone: Turquoise – keep this close by for protection, good fortune and hope
Lucky crystals: Ruby and amber
Soulmates: Aries and Sagittarius
Ruling planet: Sun
Lucky numbers: 1, 5 and 9
Lucky days: Tuesday, Friday and Sunday
Colours: Orange, yellow and red

VIRGO
(23 AUGUST–22 SEPTEMBER)

Element: Earth
Birthstone: Peridot – keep this close by for good health and harmony
Lucky crystals: Yellow aventurine and citrine
Soulmates: Taurus and Capricorn
Ruling planet: Mercury
Lucky numbers: 2, 5, 6 and 8
Lucky days: Monday, Wednesday and Thursday
Colours: Green, white, grey, yellow and orange

JUNE

See, the grass is full of stars,
Fallen in their brightness;
Hearts they have of shining gold,
Rays of shining whiteness.

Buttercups have honeyed hearts,
Bees they love the clover,
But I love the daisies' dance
All the meadows over.

Blow, O blow, you happy winds,
Singing summer's praises,
Up the field and down the field
A-dancing with the daisies.
– 'Daisy Time', Marjorie Pickthall

June is named after the Roman goddess Juno and
symbolizes marriage, childbirth and the celebration of new
horizons. This is the month we celebrate the summer solstice,
which is the longest day of the year. Flaming June is about
bringing connections together and unifying your ideas with
the seeds you have already sown. It's time to give them life
as they grow and develop, ready for you to reap later in
the year. This is a time to be grateful for all that
gives you joy.

KEY DATES

STRAWBERRY MOON

This full moon celebrates the harvesting of strawberries. Its energy is one of good fortune, optimism and generosity, so use this day to your advantage when making life plans. Spark luck and fortune in your life by keeping a piece of **tiger's eye** close by (see opposite).

10 JUNE: CELTRIC OAK TREE FESTIVAL

This Celtic festival, part of the Celtric tree calendar, celebrates the mighty oak tree. Use this time to remember how strong you are, and how well you can face problems while standing tall like the oak tree. During this festival, start a ritual to guide a long-standing project to success. Take an acorn and plant it in a pot; as the sapling grows, your project will gain momentum. Once your project reaches its goal, plant the sapling close to your home or in an area that's significant to you, and give thanks for the strength and ability with which it blessed you.

21–22 JUNE: LITHA – THE SUMMER SOLSTICE

This is the fifth of the Sabbats celebrating the Earth's journey around the sun. This pagan celebration marks the longest day of the year and is the perfect time to give thanks to the energy of the sun for the harvests to come. Embrace the day with meditations and dancing. Why not visit Stonehenge, if you live in the UK, or stream the sunset and sunrise live? Wear yellow or gold, and invite nature into your home with flowers.

CRYSTALS FOR JUNE

These crystals will support you on your quest to create a positive, summery environment.

CITRINE

Citrine welcomes joy into your life. It brings to you in abundance all that you crave and envisage, so think wisely. Citrine warms your spirit and, like the sun, will bring protection and spiritual growth to you and your loved ones.

TIGER'S EYE

Inner strength, luck and prosperity will be bestowed upon you when carrying tiger's eye. While this flashy crystal can lift your spirits, it will also calm your mind, giving you stability as you make powerful moves. This crystal dispels fear and anxiety, so is ideal to use on the path to mental wellbeing.

PYRITE

A powerful protector, pyrite will shield you from negativity, and deflect any harmful thoughts that are sent your way. Pyrite is also amazing for enhancing memory and intellect, making it perfect when studying for summer exams. Keep a piece in your office or workspace for wealth and good fortune.

RED JASPER

While you are uplifting your vibes and creating an ambience of happiness and joy, it is important to stay grounded, but also to remain fierce and confident in your endeavours. Red jasper creates balance and helps keep your feet firmly on the ground, even when your head is in the clouds.

AMETHYST

A great stress-reliever, amethyst helps to restore emotional balance. Bringing clarity and insight, this stone is perfect for keeping your mindset in check.

BLACK TOURMALINE

With its powerful grounding energy, black tourmaline is the perfect protector. Use it to dispel negative energies and feelings, and to regain focus.

PLANTS FOR JUNE

Feature these in your altar, garden or floral displays to work their energies into your day, life, spells and intentions. Place a piece of **citrine** (see page 77) in the soil of your plant pots to attract vitamin D and good vibrations this month.

ROSE

Symbolizes romance, love, beauty and courage.

POPPY

Symbolizes regeneration and eternal life.

OAK TREE

Symbolizes strength, resistance, morale and knowledge.

SYMBOLIC ANIMAL FOR JUNE

THE HORSE

The horse symbolizes determination and endurance. To harness these properties, use **pyrite** for determination or **red jasper** for endurance (see page 77).

Top to bottom: citrine (tumbles and point), pyrite (tumbles), red jasper (raw), tiger's eye (tumbles)

SUN MEDITATION RITUAL

This is particularly poignant when carried out on the summer solstice, but you can enjoy it whenever you feel like it. Remember to practise safe sun exposure: choose a cooler time of the day, such as sunset or sunrise, for an energizing and intense meditation.

You can choose to meditate by simply breathing and visualizing, or by following this guided meditation. It's best to practise at home and build up to longer meditations, so that you can embrace these moments in nature fully.

1. Find a space outside that will be both peaceful and calming. Maybe you already have a favourite meditation space in nature.

2. As you meditate, visualize the sun's rays and feel its warmth wash over you.

3. Take note of your feet on the grass, or if you have shoes on, feel the ground beneath them. If you have a **tiger's eye** (see page 77), hold this in your hands to activate your root chakra and draw the energy into the earth. The golden energy of the tiger's eye will also connect to the sun's energy and draw it closer to you.

4. Imagine the glow of the sun surrounding your aura as it invigorates you.

Simply walking in nature can be just as powerful as a seated meditation. Let your senses connect with the scent of the flowers, the sound of the leaves rustling, the feeling of the grass in between your toes; brush your fingers along the shrubs, or hold your hand on the bark of the trees as you connect with nature and the sunshine.

THE SNAKE

If you connect with or see a snake, it could be a sign that transformation in your life is imminent. This may not just be on a physical level; it could be on a spiritual or emotional level too. Trust your instincts, as you may well have been avoiding a certain path. As the snake is a reptile, it's reminding you to be careful from where – or whom – you draw your energy. Think about who you surround yourself with and who you turn to for support.

Those born in June are famous for their healing abilities. They give confidence and strength when stepping into the unknown. They will nurture you and have the very best intentions to help you become the healthiest version of yourself, physically, mentally, emotionally and spiritually.

'TO BE AWARE AND TO OBSERVE WITHOUT JUDGEMENT IS TO HAVE CLARITY AND PEACE'

It's easy to judge and impart your opinions on another, but this month, take a step back and let others create their own journeys. Focus on your own adventure and allow others to make their own discoveries as they navigate life. When you put all the effort into your own destiny, big things will happen.

Keep **amethyst** close by to balance your emotions, and **black tourmaline** to ease negative feelings (see page 77). Black tourmaline will also help you to regain focus.

THE SNAKE

JULY

Sweet July, warm July!
Month when mosses near the stream,
Soft green mosses thick and shy,
Are a rapture and a dream.
Summer Queen! whose foot the fern
Fades beneath while chestnuts burn;
I welcome thee with thy fierce love,
Gloom below and gleam above.
Though all the forest trees hang dumb,
With dense leafiness o'ercome;
Though the nightingale and thrush,
Pipe not from the bough or bush;
Come to me with thy lustrous eye,
Azure-melting westerly,
The raptures of thy face unfold,
And welcome in thy robes of gold!
Tho' the nightingale broods – 'sweet-chuck-sweet' –
And the ouzel flutes so chill,
Tho' the throstle gives but one shrilly trill
To the nightingale's 'sweet-sweet'.
– 'July', George Meredith

July was named after Julius Caesar, and was originally
the fifth month in the early Roman calendar. This month is
associated with adventure, travel and freedom. It's a time to
celebrate your wildness and freedom to explore the Earth,
with the sun's energy awakening your confidence. Take time
to connect with yourself as you embrace nature, bridging the
gaps between your mind, body and soul. July is also a month
of change and transformation, so follow your intuition and let
it lead you to your destiny.

KEY DATES

BUCK MOON

The male deer's antlers grow at this time, giving this full moon its name. This full moon centres energy around helping and supporting others, and heightens our ability to find true connections. **Prehnite** (see page 90) will protect you from absorbing other's feelings – a must for any caregivers.

3 JULY: THE FESTIVAL OF CERRIDWEN

This festival honours the Welsh mother and goddess of fertility, magic and transformation. Her name means 'white sow', and those that choose to celebrate in her honour are encouraged to use symbols such as the cauldron, rainbows and pig shapes in any ritual. Decorate your home with these symbols to alert the goddess that you are ready to embrace change and transformation, and are seeking support from the elements as you do so.

18 JULY: THE FESTIVAL OF BAD OMENS

Be aware of any signals, signs, information or intuitions that may come your way today to warn you of a situation that is best avoided. If you have a gut instinct about something or someone, today is not the day to ignore it. Trust your intuition.

CRYSTALS FOR JULY

As you embrace adventure, travel and transformation throughout July, these crystals will support you.

AMETHYST

A talisman of new adventures and travel, this vibrant crystal will protect you from misadventure and thieves. It will keep your mindset in check as you navigate new parts of the Earth, allowing you to understand deeply. It will keep stress at bay while you deal with late transport, too. A promoter of digestive health, it's perfect for carrying when trying new cuisines on your travels.

LABRADORITE

This beautiful, flashy crystal has been said to contain the Northern Lights trapped within it. It will keep you company through periods of transformation. Your instincts will be enhanced, helping you to discover and fully grasp your true life path and fortune. Labradorite is said to soothe aches and pains and is therefore a great crystal to keep in your spiritual first-aid kit.

HEMATITE

As you discover new places, spaces and people, it is important to protect your own energy and ground yourself to stay balanced. Hematite helps by creating an energy shield around you, alleviating worries and preventing the comments and opinions of others from affecting you or your mindset.

SODALITE

When navigating life's adventures, it's easy to become overwhelmed. Sodalite brings order and calmness to the mind by encouraging you to think rationally. When you need a boost of self-esteem, pop it in your pocket and it will help you to express your feelings and calm your panic and anxiety.

Left to right: hematite (tumbles), labradorite (sphere), unakite (tumbles),
amazonite (rough), sodalite (elephant), amethyst (cluster)

UNAKITE

As you sail into summer, unakite will bring you patience and alleviate the stress of organizing your trips and holidays. It will welcome kind and loving energy your way, perhaps attracting a holiday friendship. It is also one of the most popular crystals for reproductive health, so if you need support in this area, keep a piece in your pocket this month.

AMAZONITE

If there are troubles brewing, amazonite will help you to see both sides of the story clearly. It is a popular July crystal as it is associated with the sign Cancer. While the sun brings joy to many at this time, life still happens. This crystal will step in to be your support by alleviating worries and fears, dispelling negativity, and clearing energy blockages.

TIGER'S EYE

This flashy crystal will dispel worries and fears while attracting luck and prosperity. A powerful crystal for acting on your intentions, tiger's eye keeps you calm and stable while simultaneously lifting your spirits.

ONYX

Power, boldness and self-control: these are all qualities onyx will attract to you. This powerful crystal will protect and ground you, and is especially helpful during times of stress or grief.

EMERALD

Perfect for decision-making, emerald bolsters your intuition and allows you to see clearly what the outcomes of any big decisions will be. This crystal also attracts new relationships, and brings harmony, unity and compassion to existing partnerships.

PREHNITE

Caring for others is an essential part of relationships, but it can be easy to absorb others' feelings and feel them as your own. Prehnite, and **prehnite with epidote**, can help you to care for others without feeling heavy and sad.

PLANTS FOR JULY

Feature these in your altar, garden or floral displays to work their energies into your day, life, spells and intentions. **Sodalite** (see page 87) will attract healthy energy this month, as well as changing the balance of the soil if it's absorbing too much negativity from the environment.

SWEET PEA

Symbolizes blissful pleasure.

LILY

Symbolizes purity, fertility, transformation and rebirth.

MYRTLE TREE

Symbolizes love, good luck and prosperity.

SYMBOLIC ANIMAL FOR JULY

THE RAM

The ram symbolizes boldness, new beginnings, new paths and power. To harness these properties, use **onyx** for power and boldness, and **emerald** for revealing new paths (see page 90).

POSITIVE TRANSFORMATION RITUALS

To welcome a new start, embrace change and direct abundance into your life, one or all of the practices below will give you exactly the right mindset to start the process.

WRITE DOWN YOUR INTENTIONS

It could be as simple as writing 'own my own house', or 'travel to Thailand': they don't need to be pages long. Read through your list religiously once or twice a day. As the saying goes, 'the energy flows where the focus goes'. By regularly focusing on these statements of intention, you will subconsciously create energy pathways that will enable them to become reality.

EXERCISE

By exercising physically, you will be exercising your mind too. Just 30 minutes of activity will raise your confidence, energy and feelings of positivity, and will in turn help you to find new approaches for following through on your intentions. If the gym isn't your thing, then a brisk walk in nature will have resounding effects on you, both mentally and physically.

VISUALIZE

Set aside 10 minutes every day and spend them visualizing yourself *after* the transformation or change you desire has occurred, or on your new adventure. Hear the sounds and the conversations; see your new life in vivid technicolour.

CREATE A TO-DO LIST

Visualize your end goal. Now, in your mind, walk your way backwards to the very start, then list the processes that you will need to go through to get to the end. Start the very first one today. Self-belief, positivity, visualization, manifestation and spiritual guidance are so important when working towards your dreams, but actions speak louder than words. Create a healthy mindset, follow your to-do list and the rest will start falling into place.

THE DRAGONFLY

Has your life changed in the blink of an eye? Seeing or encountering the dragonfly symbolizes that transformation is on the horizon, or that it's time to release yourself from an unproductive scenario that's holding you – and your soul's progression – back.

Surrounding yourself with those born in July will be very beneficial if you find yourself in a stormy situation. July babies are fantastic at showing you the way out of dark times with confidence. Dragonflies are magical, leaving light and warmth wherever they dance, reminding you to live each moment to the fullest.

AFFIRMATION FOR JULY

'I SEE AN ABUNDANCE OF POTENTIAL IN MY LIFE, AND IN THOSE AROUND ME. OPPORTUNITIES FOR PRODUCTIVE CHANGE AND PROSPERITY ARE VISIBLE EVERYWHERE'

As you embrace adventure and travel, open your eyes to all that's around you. Remove your blinkers to see the bigger picture and notice any paths that could be passing you by. Say yes to new opportunities that excite you, and say no to those that stifle you. Be true to yourself and don't be afraid of becoming the big, beautiful butterfly that you are.

Keep **tiger's eye** (see page 90) close by to give you extra confidence, strength and a positive outlook. This flashy gem will also usher in good luck, which is always welcome when embracing new possibilities.

THE DRAGONFLY

AUGUST

August days are hot and still,
Not a breath on house or hill,
Not a breath on height or plain,
Weary travellers cry for rain;
But the children quickly find
A shady place quite to their mind;
And there all quietly they stay,
Until the sun has gone away –
August is too hot for play!
– 'August', Annette Wynne

Named after the Emperor Augustus, August is one the luckiest months. This is the ideal time to let go of old emotions, to stop judging others and to bring peace into your life. Taking these steps will allow you to better connect with your inner self, and will invite more favourable energy into your day-to-day life. This month also symbolizes regeneration, so as you shed your old mindset, be prepared to welcome a spectacular transformation as you become who you desire to be.

Those born in August tend to be honest, generous and have a strong moral compass. Keep them close by for honest answers to your dilemmas.

KEY DATES

STURGEON MOON

This full moon takes its name from the fish, which is abundant during August, and this time is therefore celebrated with a bountiful feast. Be thankful for and appreciative of all that you have, including the path that has led you to where you are now. If you aren't yet in the place you envisaged, it's time to make plans. **Aquamarine** (see opposite) will help you reflect on and tune into what you hope to achieve.

LAMMAS OR LUGHNASADH

The sixth of the Sabbats celebrating the Earth's journey around the sun, this pagan holiday falls halfway between the summer solstice (Litha, page 60) and the autumn equinox (Mabon, page 114). It is also known as the Loaf Mass Day, and encourages celebrations and get-togethers where individuals express thanks for the first harvest of the season.

13 AUGUST: HECATE DAY

A pagan celebration to honour the powerful goddess Hecate by leaving out food for wild creatures, stray animals and birds. These creatures relate to Hecate's pack of dogs, who protect her and her followers: by looking after wildlife, you are protecting her energy.

23 AUGUST: FESTIVAL OF HEPHAESTUS

A day of celebration in the name of the Greek god of fire and volcanoes. Traditionally celebrated with a meal of beef, it is said to be a lucky day to buy anything made of metal, such as new scissors, cutlery or even a car.

CRYSTALS FOR AUGUST

As you let go of past emotions and old wounds, these crystals will support you.

AQUAMARINE

Associated with tranquility and harmony, this is a wonderful crystal to keep close to you as you break free from situations that you want to let go of at the end of the season. It possesses all the healing quality of the sea, bringing you clarity as you make decisions, and helping with the transformation and rebirth of your life's path.

RHODONITE

This powerful crystal heals shock, past trauma and emotional wounds, releasing a nurturing love. It grounds your energies: carrying suppressed emotions is toxic, and this crystal will help release them in a gentle way.

GREY AGATE

A calming and soothing stone, this will bring comfort if you have suffered trauma. Grey agate is especially beneficial when letting go of past emotional turmoil, as it will help you remain calm and process everything with gentle clarity. It also relieves fatigue and removes the influence of negative thoughts.

PINK CALCITE

This crystal brings a divine peace and serenity into your life, enhancing energy flow between the head and heart. Allow pink calcite to help you heal by bringing supressed emotions to the surface and releasing them in a gentle and loving way.

Left to right: jade (worry stones), pink calcite (raw), aquamarine (tumbles), grey agate (nodule), pink rhodonite (rough point)

JADE

A lucky talisman and bringer of good fortunes, this crystal is linked to the astrological sign Virgo. It is exceptionally powerful at helping you access your dreams and manifest them into reality.

RED JASPER

If you are caught up in the current moment, red jasper will give you extra energy to help you overcome the situation with success. Boosting stamina and overall energy, this stone will help you plot, plan and organize as you move towards success and regaining control of your future.

ORANGE CALCITE

This sunshine-coloured crystal will lift your spirits, bringing you a burst of energy, creativity and joyfulness, perfect for making the most of the final month of summer. Connected to the sacral chakra, orange calcite can help to alleviate your worries and fears.

SODALITE

Bringing order and rationality, sodalite will help you to make intelligent decisions by practising objectivity. It will also support you as you use your intuition to follow through on intentions, allowing you to trust that you are making the right moves to achieve what you desire.

PLANTS FOR AUGUST

Feature these in your altar, garden or floral displays to work their energies into your day, life, spells and intentions. Any yellow crystal will promote new growth and strength in the buds as your plants flower this month.

SUNFLOWER

Symbolizes happiness, optimism, peace and devotion.

DAHLIA

Symbolizes inner strength, change and creativity.

HAZEL TREE

Symbolizes wisdom and inspiration.

AFFIRMATION FOR AUGUST

'I AM A CREATOR AND I ATTRACT MIRACLES'

You have the power and strength within you to create all you wish in your life. Be mindful when planning your next moves. Set clear goals and believe that you can achieve them.

Keep **red jasper** (see page 102) close by to keep yourself grounded, and for an extra dose of energy and courage when you feel yourself flagging or your confidence wavering.

RITUAL FOR LETTING GO

If you want to actively approach and release emotions or past traumas, this ritual will give you the empowerment that you are looking for to strive ahead.

1. Gather a piece of paper, a pen, a candle, matches and a fireproof bowl.

2. Think about the event or emotion you want to let go of and write it down.

3. Light the candle. Hold the paper in the flame until it catches fire, then place it in the fireproof bowl to burn.

4. Out loud, say: 'I no longer allow you to have power over me; I release you.'

5. Close your eyes and count your breaths. Imagine the orange firelight bathing you and filling you with confidence.

6. Thank the energy for empowering you. Give thanks that your request for release has been received and granted.

7. As you breathe in, imagine the light filling your chest and heart chakra.

8. Once the fire has burned out naturally, either wash the bowl in water, imagining the paper and hurt being washed away, or take a small amount of the fire ashes and bury them in the earth.

Remember that it's OK to seek professional support or reach out to a loved one if you are struggling to overcome past trauma and difficult emotions.

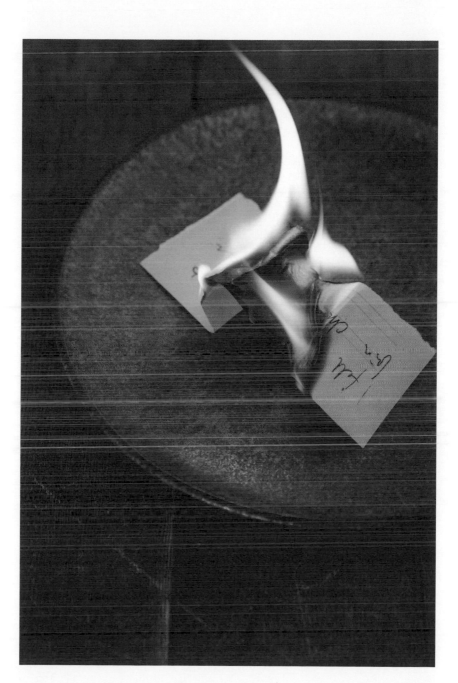

THE LION

This magnificent beast symbolizes dominance, strength and a craving for attention. If the lion crosses your path, it is a sign that you must speak out and share your truth. If you face a situation of self-doubt, it is time to summon your inner lion or lioness. You have the power within you to overcome difficulties – you just need to have a little more self-belief. Look in the mirror and see yourself as others see you.

Surround yourself with those born in August if you are looking for more empowerment in your life. Lions aren't afraid of turning their backs on the crowd and heading in a new direction. Some may call this reckless, but they've often surveyed the area and calculated all risks before heading away. They are willing to face challenges, even if they are scared; take this strength on board if you are visited by a lion.

THE MONKEY

The monkey symbolizes energy, joyfulness, knowledge and intelligence. To harness these properties, use **orange calcite** for energy and joyfulness and **sodalite** for knowledge and intelligence (see page 102).

THE LION

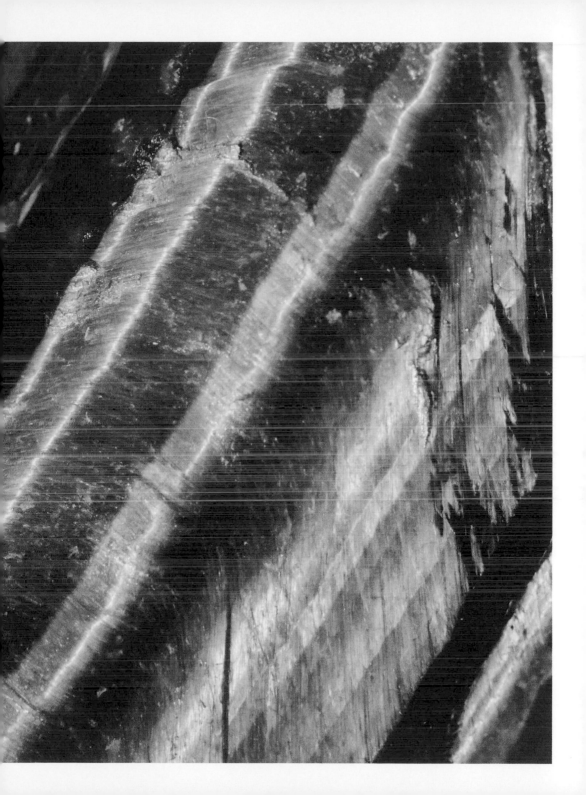

AUTUMN

IN AUTUMN, THE WEATHER STARTS TO COOL,
AND NATURE BECOMES DORMANT. THIS
SEASON LASTS FROM THE AUTUMN EQUINOX
ON AROUND 22 SEPTEMBER TO THE WINTER
SOLSTICE ON AROUND 20 DECEMBER.

Autumn reminds us to embrace the present, acknowledge our surroundings and be at one with ourselves. Everything within and around us is developing and it's important to use this season to take nourishment from the earth. Nature is rich with colour; do not miss this display of beauty. Practise self-care and take in every mental picture of your surroundings. Not only will this give you energy as the nights draw in, but it will also connect and ground you to the earth.

The autumn equinox brings us positive transformations. Darker nights may be on the way, but it's a time for planning and reflection, for looking back over your achievements and bringing the art of self-care to the forefront. Plans don't need to become dormant; in fact, it's a time of great positivity. Autumn is a time for harvest and reaping what you've sowed. Put positive affirmations in place to experience the light when you're missing it, but know that you are full of power that's being harnessed by the stars.

VIRGO
(23 AUGUST–22 SEPTEMBER)

Element: Earth
Birthstone: Peridot – keep this close by for good health and harmony
Lucky crystals: Yellow aventurine and citrine
Soulmates: Taurus and Capricorn
Ruling planet: Mercury
Lucky numbers: 2, 5, 6 and 8
Lucky days: Monday, Wednesday and Thursday
Colours: Green, white, grey, yellow and orange

LIBRA
(23 SEPTEMBER–22 OCTOBER)

Element: Air
Birthstone: Sapphire – keep this close by to attract abundance, blessings and gifts
Lucky crystals: Emerald and turquoise
Soulmates: Gemini and Aquarius
Ruling planet: Venus
Lucky numbers: 5, 6 and 9
Lucky days: Monday, Tuesday and Sunday
Colours: Blue and jade green

SCORPIO
(23 OCTOBER–21 NOVEMBER)

Element: Water
Birthstone: Opal and tourmaline – opal will amplify your intentions and energy, and bring you hope; tourmaline will offer you protection
Lucky crystals: Red coral, bloodstone and yellow aventurine
Soulmates: Cancer and Pisces
Ruling planet: Mars
Lucky numbers: 1, 2, 4 and 7
Lucky days: Monday, Tuesday, Thursday and Sunday
Colours: Red and violet

SAGITTARIUS
(23 NOVEMBER–21 DECEMBER)

Element: Fire
Birthstone: Citrine – keep this close by for abundance and joyful, warming energies
Lucky crystals: Turquoise and yellow aventurine
Soulmates: Aries and Leo
Ruling planet: Jupiter
Lucky numbers: 3, 5, 6 and 8
Lucky days: Wednesday, Thursday and Friday
Colours: Light blue, cream, white and orange

SEPTEMBER

Lo! a ripe sheaf of many golden days
Gleaned by the year in autumn's harvest ways,
With here and there, blood-tinted as an ember,
Some crimson poppy of a late delight
Atoning in its splendour for the flight
Of summer blooms and joys
This is September.
– 'September', Lucy Maud Montgomery

The name September comes from the word 'seven', as it was the originally the seventh month in the Roman calendar. September signifies a shift in the seasonal calendar as we come to the end of summer and the start of autumn. The new academic year is also upon us, which means knowledge will be flowing, giving us many of the tools we need to create a full new future. It is the month that we celebrate the autumn equinox and the harvest, and a time for being thankful for all that we have reaped after sowing our seeds in spring. The number seven makes this a month of manifestation, so it's a time to reflect and refocus our energies on tasks that will make the rest of the year the best it can possibly be.

Those born in September tend to have a more methodical approach to life. They are practical thinkers, organized and very loyal.

KEY DATES

HARVEST MOON

This refers to the time after the autumn equinox (also known as Mabon, see below) when the crops have been gathered. This full moon is brighter and lower in the sky, allowing the farmers to work longer on the land. It's time to reap the rewards for the intentions you sowed in the spring. Let the moon know you are ready to receive by simply speaking the words out loud. **Citrine** (see opposite), along with the vibrancy from the moon, will lead to master manifestation.

13 SEPTEMBER: EPULUM JOVIS

The festival of Jove, the ancient Roman god of thunder also known as Jupiter, was a lavish feast celebrated on the Ides of September. Celebrate this day by having a meal with your friends and family. Invite each other to bring a dish and give thanks for all that you have, such as food, health, finances and/or relationships. Give thanks to someone who means a lot to you and has offered you wisdom throughout the year.

17–21 SEPTEMBER: CUIVANYA

Also called the Feast of Life, this celebrates the Triple Goddess – maiden, mother, crone. Celebrate this day by wearing a triple moon symbol in the form of a brooch, necklace or crown. Wear green, brown and black, and decorate your home in these colours.

22 SEPTEMBER: MABON – THE AUTUMN EQUINOX

The seventh of the Sabbats celebrating the Earth's journey around the sun, this is a Pagan celebration marking the day and night being the same length. It is a perfect day to pause and reflect on all that you have. As the second harvest festival of the year, the emphasis is on celebrating what you have received this past season, and giving thanks for the abundance that is already in your life, as well as that which is on its way. If you feel that life is unbalanced and you are spending too much time working, too much time with negative people or too much time partying, now is the time to rebalance. Refocus your energies and welcome more of the positive into your existence.

CRYSTALS FOR SEPTEMBER

As you reflect, these crystals will give you the support you need to make wise decisions.

SUNSTONE

Radiant and full of energy, this crystal carries the healing energies of personal power and the ability to reflect with clarity, freedom and enhanced consciousness. It will give you the strength you need to make decisions with openness and gratitude. If you are feeling tension in your stomach, sunstone will help ease this sensation. Perfect for those back-to-school nerves.

AMETHYST

This powerful crystal will balance your energies emotionally, spiritually and physically, and calm your stress levels as you make decisions about where you need to put more effort into in your life, making it a perfect crystal to use when studying. It will give you clarity so you can see other points of view more rationally. Amethyst is also said to reduce inflammation and speed up healing – perfect for playground scrapes for the children in your life.

CARNELIAN

Motivation in crystal form, this ball of energy will galvanize you as you pursue new goals and face a new season (and, if you are a student, the new academic year). As you hold the crystal, imagine its orange energy surrounding your whole aura, giving it a supercharge, like a battery.

CITRINE

Known as the merchant's stone, citrine brings clarity to your decision-making. Associated with Virgo, it is particularly powerful when held by someone of this zodiac sign. Not only does citrine lift your spirits and embody confidence, it will also help you to feel more grateful for all you have and have achieved.

Left to right: citrine (tumbles), green aventurine (point), amethyst (cluster), rose quartz (point), sunstone (point), carnelian (pebble), black tourmaline (raw)

GREEN AVENTURINE

As nature starts to hibernate, it is human nature to do the same. The darker nights lead to the desire to stay home more. Though this is what we may need at this time, it can sometimes lead to fatigue and a lack of motivation. Green aventurine sparks your social energy and awakens the adventurer within you. It also keeps the flame burning on your fun-loving side.

ROSE QUARTZ

If you are feeling unsettled and your nerves are frayed, this beautiful pink gem will provide inner peace and attract unconditional friendships to deepen your support circle. This crystal not only attracts love, but also teaches you to be loving and kind to yourself.

BLACK TOURMALINE

If you are surrounded by problems to which you can't seem to grasp the answers, black tourmaline will unlock your logic and allow you to think methodically. Carrying this crystal will also protect you. It has a strong grounding energy that will clear negative vibes and strengthen the body and soul. Perfect for disruptive workplaces or classrooms.

AGATE

Beneficial when it comes to finding answers, this crystal will help you on your quest for balance. Keep it close by to support you through emotional trauma, and to dispel feelings of negativity and guilt.

RED JASPER

Perfect for building strength and courage, this crystal will keep you grounded while supporting you to act with confidence.

CLEAR QUARTZ

Attracting optimism, energy and clarity of mind, clear quartz is perfect for visualizing and manifesting your hopes, wishes and dreams. This crystal is also said to be a master healer.

PLANTS FOR SEPTEMBER

Feature these in your altar, garden or floral displays to work their energies into your day, life, spells and intentions. **Black tourmaline** (see opposite) will repel pests and prevent insects from feeding on the plant this month. It's also highly protective for the room in which the plant is placed, as it is said to absorb energies from electronics which emit EMFs (Electromagnetic Fields).

ASTER

Symbolizes love, wisdom and faith.

CHRYSANTHEMUM

Symbolizes inner happiness, honesty and friendship.

HORSE CHESTNUT TREE

Symbolizes hope, luck and freedom.

SYMBOLIC ANIMAL FOR SEPTEMBER

THE BEAR

The bear symbolizes strength, family, courage and health. To harness these properties, use **red jasper** for strength and courage, and **clear quartz** for health and a higher connection to your family (see page 118).

BALANCE RITUAL

Use this ritual to reconnect with nature. When leading a busy lifestyle, it is easy to feel like you're gliding through life, but by slowing down, you will feel connected to the earth. In turn, you will feel more grounded and balanced. Keeping **amethyst** (see page 115) with you as you practise this ritual will support you, while also allowing you to be at your best day to day. Complete this on the equinox for a truly wonderful experience.

1. Gather a piece of paper and a pen and step outside – head to your favourite nature point, if you can.

2. Stand with your bare feet on the grass. If this isn't possible, imagine the *sensation* of your feet on the ground.

3. Visualize the roots from the grass beneath you, entwining with your feet.

4. Out loud or in your mind, say: 'I am grounded and balanced, and supported by nature.'

5. Stand or sit for 10 minutes, focusing on the sounds of the birds or trees. Feel your feet on the ground; feel the weight of your body on the ground, connecting to the earth's energy.

6. Give thanks to the earth for its nourishing and balancing energy.

7. Now take a piece of paper and write down all the things that you would like to either spend less – or more – time on. Put them in order of importance and mindfully approach each item, one at a time, not visiting the next until the last is resolved.

THE WOLF

The powerful wolf crossing your path could indicate that you have an appetite for freedom, and a fear of being let down by those who mean the most to you. It's important to pay attention to what your intuition is telling you. It could also signify that you don't trust yourself. Be careful of your raw emotions – they could become unbalanced – so passionately put all that energy into your endeavours, in order to avoid a confrontation that you may live to regret.

If you are looking for protection, surround yourself with people born in September; they make good team mates and will know how to lighten the mood with a little fun when needed. They make loyal friends, but can need some guidance from time to time.

'I GIVE MYSELF THE CARE AND ATTENTION THAT I DESERVE'

When seeking balance in life, it's easy to feel that we should be making more of an effort with our family, our friends and our livelihoods, when really we should be practising more self-care and self-nourishment. Don't feel guilty for putting yourself first; you cannot pour from an empty cup.

Keep **agate** (see page 118) close by to help you overcome any guilt, emotional trauma and negativity on your quest for balance and healing.

THE WOLF

OCTOBER

October is the treasurer of the year,
And all the months pay bounty to her store;
The fields and orchards still their tribute bear,
And fill her brimming coffers more and more.

But she, with youthful lavishness,
Spends all her wealth in gaudy dress,
And decks herself in garments bold
Of scarlet, purple, red, and gold.

She heedeth not how swift the hours fly,
But smiles and sings her happy life along;
She only sees above a shining sky;
She only hears the breezes' voice in song.
– From 'October', Paul Laurence Dunbar

The name October comes from the Latin word 'Octo' which means eight, as this used to be the eighth month in the Roman calendar. The days are darkening, the leaves are falling and the earth starts to descend into slumber. This is a month of wealth, prosperity and peace. Abundance flows as the farmers finish collecting their crops to sell them at market. It's a wonderful time to seize opportunities, with endless rewards if these are acted upon in a timely manner. This is a month of magic and mystery, so don't be afraid to try new tricks.

Those born in October are kind-hearted and make good friends. Born peacemakers, they are also hard workers and have a determined personality.

KEY DATES

HUNTER'S MOON

This full moon is so named after hunting season: deer and foxes are unable to hide in the now-bare fields, and the bright skies help with visibility. Your inner warrior will be activated during this full moon. Use this time wisely and carefully, as you'll be more volatile, but will also have more confidence to stand up for yourself and your beliefs. Keep **black tourmaline** (see opposite) close to you to help you gain strength while grounding and settling heightened spirits.

4 OCTOBER: ANIMAL BLESSING DAY

Celebrated on the feast day of St Francis of Assisi, this special day is about making your pets understand how loved they are. Take them on a long walk, prepare their favourite food, thank them for choosing you as their guardian and bless them with good health and comfort. Remember that you get back what you put into the world: give your time at a local animal rescue centre or look after a friend's pet for benefits to your own wellbeing.

9 OCTOBER: FESTIVAL OF FELICITAS

The Roman goddess Felicitas is associated with changing your luck when you adjust your behaviour towards yourself and others. This is a day for spreading cheer and kindness, for making others feel wonderful about themselves and making their day a little brighter. A simple smile, a 'good morning' or a 'thank you' to a stranger, or a message of gratitude to a friend, will ensure kindness and good fortune are spread and sent back to you tenfold.

31 OCTOBER: HALLOWEEN

Celebrated the night before All Saints' Day, Halloween is a fun celebration with elaborate costumes, pumpkins, haunted houses, trick or treating and games.

31 OCTOBER–1 NOVEMBER: SAMHAIN

The eighth of the Sabbats celebrating the Earth's journey around the sun, this pagan celebration marks the end of the harvest. Samhain also symbolizes the start of winter and is the witchy New Year. On these days, it is said that the veil between the worlds of the living and the dead is especially thin, allowing the dead to visit and communicate with their living loved ones. Celebrations include bonfires, dancing and feasts, and a supper honouring ancestors.

CRYSTALS FOR OCTOBER

Welcome abundance into your life with the following crystals.

CITRINE

The yellow energy of citrine attracts joy and wealth, so keep this crystal in the money corner of your home, the furthest left corner from your front door. Ensure the area is clutter free to allow the energy to flow freely. Citrine will also lift and improve your physical energy.

PYRITE

This shimmering crystal creates wealth and success, nurtures creativity and helps to inspire money-making ideas, meaning it's perfect for the businessperson within you. If you are feeling depleted after an illness, pyrite will give you fresh vitality.

MOOKAITE

As the nights darken and the days get colder, this energetic stone will bring you warmth, enlightenment and optimism. It's aligned with spiritual health – perfect for Samhain and Halloween – and encourages the acceptance of change and emotional growth.

LAPIS LAZULI

The colour of the night sky, with golden flecks running through it like stars, lapis lazuli is perfect for bringing harmony into your home life during the darker nights. The stone of truth and friendship, it encourages healthier, deeper relationships. It is also a great psychic-attack protector, perfect for Samhain and Halloween, when spells and intentions are cast in abundance.

BLACK TOURMALINE

Like all black crystals, this powerful crystal is a protective powerhouse: perfect for keeping you grounded during Samhain and Halloween.

Left to right: pyrite (tumbles), black obsidian (sphere), lapiz lazuli (point), mookaite (heart), orange calcite (sphere), citrine (point and tumbles)

BLACK OBSIDIAN

Formed by cooling volcanic lava, this crystal contains the ability to sever karmic ties and cut cords with others, making it highly favourable for use during spellwork. A powerful cleanser of psychic smog, it will keep you grounded and protected during Samhain and Halloween.

ORANGE CALCITE

A generator of joy and happiness, orange calcite is said to ease the symptoms of Seasonal Affective Disorder (SAD) by bringing joy and sunshine to the carrier or wearer. As the nights darken, keeping it close by will help you keep a sense of light and physical energy.

GARNET

Symbolizing strength and courage, garnet is the perfect crystal to use when creating positive changes. This is a crystal of prosperity, helping you to welcome abundance into your life.

ROSE QUARTZ

Full of loving energy, rose quartz will deepen your relationships and attract love and relationships to your life. During the colder months, it's especially important to be kind to yourself: rose quartz will allow you to practise self-love.

SMOKY QUARTZ

Smoky quartz neutralizes negative vibrations and dispels fears – perfect for Halloween. Keep it close to quieten your fears and worries, and ease any pressure that you have felt building up.

BLACK ONYX

Black onyx is another black crystal, perfect for the shorter days and cold, dark nights. It will keep you grounded and protected during Samhain and Halloween, and will support you as you practise discipline and self-control.

PLANTS FOR OCTOBER

Feature these in your altar, garden or floral displays to work their energies into your day, life, spells and intentions. Orange crystals, such as **orange calcite** (see page 130), will welcome vitality into the plant's roots this month. Plant them right next to the stalk, around half a centimetre down.

RED HOT POKER

Symbolizes good fortune.

COSMOS

Symbolizes balance and tranquility.

MARIGOLD

Symbolizes strength and power.

RED MAPLE TREE

Symbolizes practical magic and generosity.

AFFIRMATION FOR OCTOBER

'I BELIEVE IN MY DREAMS, THE MAGIC I AM CREATING AND ALL THAT I AM'

The key to getting all that you want is believing you can have it. Self-belief is one of the most important gifts that you can give yourself. Look in the mirror and repeat, 'I can, I will, I am.' Use these words at the beginning of any sentence in place of 'I can't'.

Use **garnet** (see page 130) to boost your confidence; it will work with your lower chakras to activate and align this energy for your highest good.

RITUAL FOR WELCOMING AND HONOURING PASSED LOVED ONES

This ritual is to be practised on Halloween or Samhain, when the veil to the other world is thinning, allowing spirits to visit more freely.

1. Gather a black candle, seasonal foods such as pumpkins, squashes and fresh vegetables, and a few special photos of your passed loved ones.

2. On 31 October, light the candle and place it in the window or by your front door. This will show your passed ancestors that you are inviting friendly spirits to visit. If your altar is by a window or door, and can be seen from the outside, this would be a wonderful space to place the candle.

3. Place a plate of seasonal food at your dining table in honour of your visitor. Include their favourite food, if you know it.

4. Place the photos of your loved ones on the table as a clear signal of who you would like to come and visit.

5. Out loud, say: 'Friendly spirits, we open our house for you to visit; loved ones passed, we send you this light to guide you. Please come and stay for a while until the sun rises in the morning.'

6. You may not see them, but you will be aware of their presence. Look out for a favourite smell, song or dream. It will be clear to you when they have been.

Do not be disheartened if your loved ones are unable to make themselves known. Just know that they were there during this time, and left loving energy in their wake.

THE FALCON

A bird of vision and success, dreaming of or seeing a falcon is a sign that it's time to share your wisdom with others to guide them to the same successes you yourself have enjoyed. Don't be afraid to share with others; believe in yourself. Your knowledge will be gratefully received, and you will start a ripple effect of good energy and teachings. Your force is a bright light. Those born in October reiterate that using your proverbial life tools for personal and group tasks will bring soaring success. Make the effort to trust and believe in yourself more this month.

You will know if you have a falcon in your life, as they will demonstrate great support and motivation when you need it the most, especially when you are going through difficult changes. Falcons just need to stay grounded from time to time, so carrying **smoky quartz** or **black onyx** (see page 130) will be beneficial.

SYMBOLIC ANIMAL FOR OCTOBER

THE DOG

The dog symbolizes unconditional love, loyalty and protection. To harness these properties, use **rose quartz** for love, **lapis lazuli** for loyalty and **black tourmaline** for protection (see pages 127 and 130).

THE FALCON

NOVEMBER

Fall, leaves, fall; die, flowers, away;
Lengthen night and shorten day;
Every leaf speaks bliss to me
Fluttering from the autumn tree.
I shall smile when wreaths of snow
Blossom where the rose should grow;
I shall sing when night's decay
Ushers in a drearier day.
– 'Fall, Leaves, Fall', Emily Brontë

Dark, sparkling nights of midnight blue and twinkling stars, November is a month of magic. Its name comes from the Latin *'novem'*, meaning nine, as it was once the ninth month of the Roman calendar. It is the month of gratitude; by practising thanks and looking outwardly at all you are grateful for, you can enhance your life, both mentally and spiritually. It's a time of light and joy; a time to balance the darker nights by igniting your passions.

Those born in November are usually calm and in control of their emotions – unless provoked and prodded. Stand back if you push a November baby to the edge! Their passions run deep, and those born during this month are often generous to a fault.

KEY DATES

BEAVER MOON

This full moon is so named because beavers are active during the month of November, busily building their winter dams. Use this time for self-care, relaxation and reflection. **Amethyst** (see opposite) will support and calm you.

1–2 NOVEMBER: DAY OF THE DEAD (*DÍA DE LOS MUERTOS*)

This heartfelt festival honouring passed loved ones is famously celebrated throughout Mexico and Latin America. On this day, people gather to honour their ancestors with traditional foods, including *pan de muerto*. They dress in eye-catching dress and make offerings at a decorated altar. Decorations include candles, photos and colourful sugar skulls known as *calaveras*.

5 NOVEMBER: GUY FAWKES NIGHT

Celebrated in the UK, this festival marks the failure of the Gunpowder Plot of 1605. Traditions include the lighting of bonfires, fireworks and the eating of cozy, autumnal foods such as baked potatoes, hot dogs, toffee apples and toasted marshmallows. Parkin, a gingerbread Bonfire Night cake, is traditional in the north of England.

12 NOVEMBER: FESTIVAL OF ODIN

Celebrated by pagans, the Festival of Odin is a great opportunity to reconnect with nature by taking a walk or enjoying any green space that is close to your home. Decorate your home with greenery and wood, notably oak, holly and ivy. Odin was the great magician amongst the gods, so embrace the magic of nature. Meditate, create art, exercise – whatever activity you feel connected to, go with it.

16 NOVEMBER: CROSSROAD NIGHT

Also known as Hecate's Night, this is a pagan festival night to honour the goddess, and to embrace your intuition and wisdom. Wear black and silver and plan a night of divine calm and meditation. Seek knowledge in books and oracle or tarot cards.

CRYSTALS FOR NOVEMBER

Welcome gratitude and thankfulness into your life with the following crystals.

AMETHYST

This beautiful crystal is frequently used for meditation. With its power to calm the mind, it transmutes negativity into positivity and higher vibrations, helping us to be more present in our day-to-day lives and to see the blessings and the beauty of our surroundings, everywhere we go.

EMERALD

A stone of acceptance, emerald enables us to calm any nagging voices that focus on the negative. It gives us the ability to embrace our emotions and spirituality and see things from a place of happiness, love and understanding.

CITRINE

This sunny crystal helps us appreciate the joy in the smallest of things, as well as helping us to see the opportunities that might usually pass us by. Citrine gives you the strength to embrace the ups and downs of life, and imbues you with a zest for life that will then attract more warmth and positivity to you.

CLEAR QUARTZ

If you are feeling stuck in a rut and hold cynical views on the world, clear quartz will steer you towards a more optimistic mindset, giving you confidence that everything will work out, as well as gratitude that you have got through difficult experiences. It is also great for a burst of energy.

MALACHITE

The essence of joy, this stone brings ease during times of change and gives you the insight needed for personal growth.

CHRYSOCOLLA

The encourager of gratefulness, chrysocolla gives you the perspective to see things from a place of love and forgiveness. It connects your head to your heart, and helps you to take the good from situations rather than becoming overwhelmed by the shadows and gloom.

MOSS AGATE

As the nights grow longer and the days get colder, November is a time for introspection. Moss agate will allow you to analyse areas of your life where you can make changes to move closer to your goals. This crystal will also allow you to identify past events you need to move on from – perfect for leaving behind the old and making way for the new at the end of the season.

MOONSTONE

The crystal of new starts, moonstone promotes growth: use it to nurture and support your own endeavours, or even use it with your plants (see page 147).

ORANGE CALCITE

This nurturing crystal brings joy and happiness. Keep it close or use it during meditation for a boost of sunshine energy.

Top to bottom: clear quartz (point), chrysocolla (pebble), moss agate (point), malachite (freeform), citrine (point and tumbles), amethyst (cluster)

GRATITUDE STONE EXERCISE

This exercise is great for everyone, but is especially beneficial when shared with the children in your life, be they your own children, young nieces and nephews or younger siblings.

1. Set aside some time to go for a walk. While you are out and about, choose a rock or stone: choose one that will fit in your pocket or is small enough to be carried around.

2. Give thanks to the rock for making itself known to you, ready to be used to help you achieve your greater good.

3. Decorate the rock with a word, phrase, name or design that will calm you and remind you of what you are grateful for.

4. Carry it with you and, in times of need – or when you simply see it, even by pure accident – you will be reminded of how thankful you feel. Not only is this a fun and creative exercise, it also helps you connect with the present moment and improves your sense of wellbeing, compassion and gratitude.

THE CAMEL

An animal of means, the camel always has something tucked away for a rainy day and is the symbol of a pragmatic saver. However, meeting the camel can also be a sign that it's time to replenish your soul and do something you love. Whatever you set your mind to will lead to prosperity, affluence, love and success, as your dedication and focus on your goals are admirable. The camel also encourages you to focus on your desired outcomes with gratitude and thankfulness for what is to come.

You will know if you have a camel in your life, as they will be upfront and straight with you. They are unable to tell white lies and can only voice the truth – they hate gossip. They can be demanding, but they will also care for and love you with every piece of their heart.

THE PIG

The pig symbolizes thoughtfulness, fairness, attentiveness and abundance. To harness these properties, use **malachite** for fairness and attentiveness, and **citrine** for abundance (see page 139).

THE CAMEL

END OF THE DAY GRATITUDE EXERCISE

This may be a fairly simple exercise, but don't underestimate its importance. It will have an ever-expanding effect on your mindset and life.

1. Choose a blank notebook and a pen or some pens.

2. Set aside 10 minutes when you know you won't be interrupted.

3. Focus on all the things that have made you feel thankful or happy today. Examples could be someone opening a door for you, a neighbour saying good morning, receiving happy news, finding a special gift for someone, or noticing new flowers that are growing.

4. Take time to write these down on one page. Start the list with the words 'I am grateful for'. Add drawings, if you like.

5. Once you have finished the list, write the date and sign your name. Pop a **clear quartz** or **citrine** (see page 139) on your book to amplify the warm, happy energy that is vibrating from the words within it. You could also revisit the book at the end of the year as a reflection exercise, giving thanks for all your accomplishments.

Regularly practising gratitude in this way has been shown to ease symptoms of anxiety and contribute to a sense of wellbeing. I've suggested using a notebook as you can then reflect on past joys, and by revisiting them you can once more tap in to the lovely feelings that you experienced at the time.

PLANTS FOR NOVEMBER

Feature these in your altar, garden or floral displays to work their energies into your day, life, spells and intentions. **Moonstone** (see page 140) will promote new growth as and when you need to cut your plants back. This crystal tolerates water, so placing it directly in the soil is fine.

ALSTROEMERIA

Symbolizes achieving aspirations and devotion to friendship.

CHRYSANTHEMUM

Symbolizes happiness and joy.

HOLLY

Symbolizes peace and goodwill.

WINTER-FLOWERING CHERRY BLOSSOM TREE

Symbolizes pleasantness, goodness and good fortune.

AFFIRMATION FOR NOVEMBER

'I AM FULL OF ENERGY AND OPTIMISM. I AM READY TO FIND JOY'

During the darker months, it is common to feel lacking in energy. Use this affirmation to empower and reignite your sacral and solar plexus chakras. Allow yourself to feel any joy, even the smallest glimmer. Practise gratitude daily and focus on the good in your life as you navigate each day.

Use **orange calcite** (see page 140) for a boost of sunshine when you need it the most. Meditate or just keep it close by, or hold it in your hand while visualizing the sun's rays bathing you.

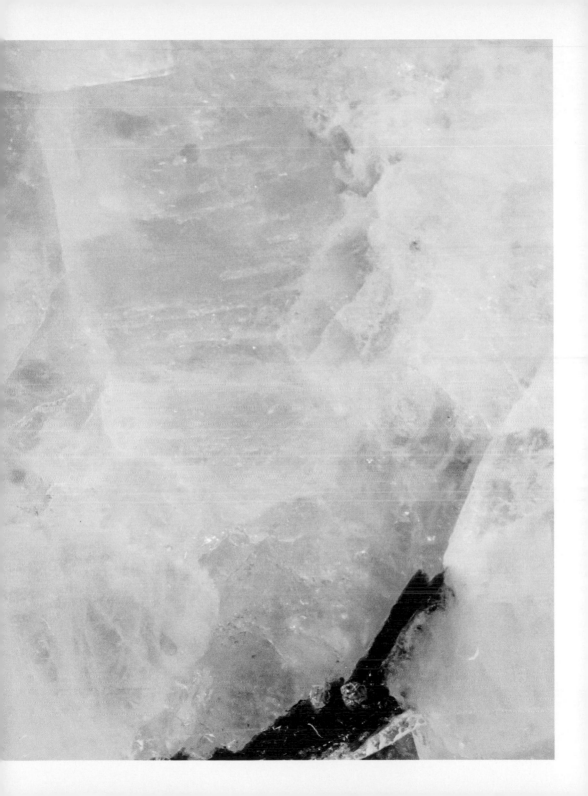

WINTER

THE COLDEST SEASON IS UPON US, WITH
ITS CRISP DAYS AND FROSTY MORNINGS,
WHEN NATURE SLEEPS AND THE EARTH
HIBERNATES BELOW FALLEN LEAVES AND
POWDERY SNOW. BEGINNING AT THE WINTER
SOLSTICE, THE SHORTEST DAYLIGHT DAY
ON AROUND 20 DECEMBER, AND ENDING
AT THE SPRING EQUINOX, ON AROUND
20 MARCH, WINTER IS A TIME FOR REST
AND REFLECTION.

Don't be hard on yourself for taking time for you and indulging in self-care. It's key to be at one with yourself and let your soul nourish itself so you're ready for spring. Healing and storing energy will help bring new ideas to life; after the darkness, the sun will return.

The winter solstice symbolizes darkness and the need for patience as we wait for the light to return. Use this patience as you grow within, taking time to relax, be still and nurture yourself before the spring equinox arrives and all starts to awaken. Spend time with loved ones and enjoy the winter celebrations, but be mindful that you may feel your emotions more strongly during this time. Allow your emotions to guide you as you start to make plans; let your intuition lead you to new and exciting ideas as the sunlight returns. However, don't put pressure on yourself to rush. Being still and calm is important.

WINTER ZODIAC SIGNS

SAGITTARIUS
(23 NOVEMBER–21 DECEMBER)

Element: Fire
Birthstone: Citrine – keep this close by for abundance and joyful, warming energies
Lucky crystals: Turquoise and yellow aventurine
Soulmates: Aries and Leo
Ruling planet: Jupiter
Lucky numbers: 3, 5, 6 and 8
Lucky days: Wednesday, Thursday and Friday
Colours: Light blue, cream, white and orange

CAPRICORN
(22 DECEMBER–20 JANUARY)

Element: Earth
Birthstone: Garnet – keep this crystal close by to relight the fire in any relationship
Lucky crystals: Black onyx and emerald
Soulmates: Taurus and Virgo
Ruling planet: Saturn
Lucky numbers: 6, 8 and 9
Lucky days: Tuesday and Friday
Colours: Black, purple and khaki

AQUARIUS
(21 JANUARY–18 FEBRUARY)

Element: Air
Birthstone: Amethyst – keep this close by to stay in touch with your intuition
Lucky crystal: Opal
Soulmates: Gemini and Libra
Ruling planets: Saturn and Uranus
Lucky numbers: 2, 3, 7 and 9
Lucky days: Monday, Tuesday, Thursday and Friday
Colour: Electric blue

PISCES
(19 FEBRUARY–20 MARCH)

Element: Water
Birthstone: Aquamarine – keep this close by for emotional clarity
Lucky crystals: Yellow jasper and yellow sapphire
Soulmates: Cancer and Scorpio
Ruling planets: Jupiter and Neptune
Lucky numbers: 3 and 7
Lucky days: Tuesday, Thursday and Sunday
Colours: Turquoise, green and aqua

DECEMBER

The night is darkening round me,
The wild winds coldly blow;
But a tyrant spell has bound me
And I cannot, cannot go.
The giant trees are bending
Their bare boughs weighed with snow.
And the storm is fast descending,
And yet I cannot go.
Clouds beyond clouds above me,
Wastes beyond wastes below;
But nothing drear can move me;
I will not, cannot go.
– 'Spellbound', Emily Brontë

The festive season is in full swing. This is a month of merriment, candles, fairy lights, gift-giving and celebration. December represents both endings and beginnings. It is a month of unity and trust within groups and families, with gatherings arranged to reminisce about the completed year and celebrate the seasonal festivities.

Those born in December tend to be down-to-earth and friendly, with a sense of motivation to help, teach and inspire those around them. Highly organized, they have a treasure trove of talents, and come to the rescue when you need them the most. You will know if you encounter a December baby, as they will have an air of spirituality about them, as well as an enthusiasm for everything they do. They have a genuine excitement about learning and teaching others new skills, especially when it comes to sports and literature.

KEY DATES

COLD MOON

With the coming of winter and the cold, short days and longer nights, this full moon symbolizes the end of the autumn. Full of spiritual revelation and purpose, the Cold Moon signifies renewal of spirit. Get ready to reset and re-evaluate as you head into the new year. **Moonstone** (see page 156) will awaken your mind's eye, helping to direct you towards your chosen path. It will also support you as you embark on new beginnings.

16 DECEMBER: FESTIVAL OF SAPIENTIA

Sapientia is the Roman goddess of wisdom and philosophy. On this day, open your mind to new subjects, or enrol on that course you've been thinking about. Spiritual development is also encouraged, with the reading of cards, palms or books. Let your creativity flow. Embody Sapientia by reorganizing your study space or bookshelf to allow the energy to flow freely. Try placing a **sodalite** (see page 158) in your study area.

21 DECEMBER: WINTER SOLSTICE

This celebration of the shortest day of the year celebrates the presence of spirit and the power of faith and hope. It's a time to start something new and to manifest your hopes and dreams. Though you won't necessarily see the fruits of your labour just yet, you are encouraged to take energy from the new sun to practise discipline and stay focused on your path to success.

21 DECEMBER–1 JANUARY: YULE

The first of the Sabbats celebrating the Earth's journey around the sun. The pagan name for the winter solstice, Yule is a celebration of the newborn Sun god and the welcoming of the return of light. It is a powerful time for rebirth and ending that which no longer serves you.

25 DECEMBER: CHRISTMAS DAY

A traditional Christian holiday for celebrating the birth of Jesus, celebrated with the giving and receiving of gifts. In Europe, Christmas is often celebrated on 24 December. Celebrations and traditional foods vary by country; turkey, roast potatoes, Yorkshire puddings and all the trimmings are eaten for Christmas dinner in the UK. While gifts are lovely, use this day as a time to offer kindness, gestures of goodwill and support to others. Invite loved ones to celebrate each other's joys from throughout the year and reflect with gratitude.

31 DECEMBER: NEW YEAR'S EVE

A celebration of seeing out the old year and bringing in the new. Traditions vary by country, but this is typically a day of setting new resolutions and goals for the year ahead. Take the time to be proud of your personal achievements. What have you learned? What can you take forwards, and what can you leave behind as you start a new chapter? Just remember to be kind to yourself and give yourself credit where it is due.

CRYSTALS FOR DECEMBER

During this month of endings, new beginnings, changes and intention-setting, these crystals will support you.

RAINBOW MOONSTONE

This beautiful gem will strengthen your intuition so you can better process your feelings when deciding what to move on from and what to leave behind. It will also support you when thinking about the future and the decisions ahead.

MOONSTONE

Strongly connected to the moon and new beginnings, this will remind you of the strength you have deep inside, helping you to deal with the waves of emotions you may encounter as you begin a new chapter in your life. It will nurture you as you embark on a journey of inner growth and inspire you to take the first step while providing a sense of calm.

MOSS AGATE

Change is inevitable; though we all know this, it can still bring with it feelings of discomfort. Moss agate gives you a clear focus, as well as a sense of positivity and self-belief in the decisions you have made. Keeping a piece close by will also help keep your immune system healthy and work to lower fevers associated with cold and flu – perfect for December healing.

LABRADORITE

A powerful protector, labradorite will create a shield for your aura as you set your intentions, protecting you against the negativity of the world. This is ideal when heading into the new year with a fresh approach. It is also a useful companion during times of change, giving you strength and perseverance.

RED TIGER'S EYE

Perfect for imbuing you with energy, passion and strength, this crystal will dispel any fears that may be holding you back, and provides useful insights.

Top to bottom: labradorite (sphere), moonstone (pebbles), pink agate (nodule), jade (worry stone), emerald (rough), rainbow moonstone (point), sodalite (elephant)

EMERALD

Perfect for December Capricorns, emerald allows us to tune into both our feelings and our intuition. Emerald is also an ideal crystal for letting go of negative thoughts, making room for love and understanding.

SODALITE

As you tap into your intuition to help you make decisions, resolutions and intentions, sodalite will have your back. It encourages rational thought and objectivity so that you don't make decisions out of haste. It also raises your self-esteem, self-acceptance and self-trust.

PINK AGATE

December can be a time of heightened emotions. Keeping this agate close by will offer you energy and courage, and it's also a highly calming and soothing stone – the perfect combination for party season if you are more introvert than extrovert.

JADE

Good fortune and luck await with jade by your side. Jade will alert you to your life's purpose, meaning that new adventures and opportunities could appear out of the blue – an exciting stone to help you prepare for the new year.

AMBER

If you find family gatherings stressful, especially if you only meet at seasonal celebrations, keep this crystal close by. Better still, wear it on a chain to absorb negativity and give you sunshine and strength around energy vampires.

ROSE QUARTZ

Associated with the heart chakra, rose quartz is perfect for nurturing love and relationships. In the winter months, use this crystal to build a loving relationship with yourself, and don't forget to show yourself kindness, respect and gratitude.

BLACK TOURMALINE

This powerful crystal is a talisman of protection and purification, repelling negative energy – the perfect companion for the dark months of winter.

PLANTS FOR DECEMBER

Feature these in your altar, garden or floral displays to work their energies into your day, life, spells and intentions. **Pink agate** (see page 158) will nurture plants as they lie dormant until spring.

POINSETTIA

Symbolizes good cheer, success and good fortune.

NARCISSUS

Symbolizes creativity, forgiveness, inner reflection and vitality.

AMARYLLIS

Symbolizes pride and determination.

THE BIRCH TREE

Symbolizes rebirth, new beginnings and growth.

SYMBOLIC ANIMAL FOR DECEMBER

THE RAT

The rat symbolizes strength, fertility and wealth. To harness these properties, use **red tiger's eye** for strength, **moonstone** for fertility and **jade** for wealth (see pages 156 and 158).

FESTIVE YULE AND SOLSTICE TASKS

These simple projects and rituals will allow you to honour your own spirituality at the same time as having fun with family. Take the time to nurture your wellbeing throughout the month of December, and give time to self-care. Remember, it's OK to say no and put your mental health first.

CREATE A NATURAL GARLAND

Gather popcorn, dried cranberries and raisins. Thread them together to create a natural garland in a beautiful offering that will honour Mother Nature and the Triple Goddess. Once the celebrations are over, remove any food from the thread and place in your garden for birds and animals to enjoy. Alternatively, create an outdoor edible tree for animals using seed ornaments, dried citrus, fruits, berries, peanut butter, popcorn and cranberries.

AWAKEN YOUR WINTER KNOWLEDGE

Use this time of reflection to read solstice and Yule-inspired books.

MAKE ORANGE POMANDERS

Gather oranges, cloves and a cocktail stick or toothpick. Use a citrus zester to create patterns in the orange, if you like, then pierce holes in the orange with the cocktail stick. Place a clove in each hole and enjoy the festive aroma.

RELEASE AND LET GO

Light a fire with a Yule log. If you don't have one, then a small fire outside in a fireproof vessel works just as well. On a piece of paper, write down all that you wish to unburden yourself of. You can do this alone or with a group, if you prefer. Throw the paper into the fire, while saying: 'I release what no longer serves me,' and watch the darkness turn to light.

MAKE SOLSTICE LANTERNS

Gather tissue paper, scissors, craft glue, clean jam jars, a few small leaves and tealights. Cut out moon and star shapes from the tissue paper and glue them to the outsides of the jars, along with the leaves. Once the jars are decorated to your liking, seal with a layer of glue and allow to dry. Once fully dried, place a tealight inside each jar, then light. Embrace the warm glow and give thanks as you welcome back the light into your life and home.

DECEMBER'S ANIMAL PERSONALITY

THE OWL

This magnificent creature represents those wise, knowledgeable people who have the ability to navigate life's darkest moments. Seeing an owl is a sign that your spirituality has awoken. Your awareness of the lunar cycles is strengthening, so be sure to embrace the moon and its messages and guidance at this time. Listen to your inner voice and embrace your inner god or goddess as you face your shadows and fears. Release the past and let go of burdens that hold you back. Move beyond them to find your true happiness.

You will know if you have an owl in your life, as they are observant, and able to join the dots when discussing mysteries and cryptic puzzles. They remember the finer details and enjoy working alone. They may not talk a lot in a group of people, but when they do, they speak with wisdom, clarity and purpose.

AFFIRMATION FOR DECEMBER

'CHANGE IS GOOD FOR ME; I DON'T GIVE POWER OR ENERGY TO THINGS THAT MAKE ME FEEL BAD'

Letting things go and moving on is easier said than done, but by giving your time, power and energy to the situations and areas in your life that lift your spirits instead of those which drain you, you'll find yourself naturally gravitating towards things that make you feel good about yourself. These small steps are just the start you need.

Rose quartz (see page 158) will work with your heart chakra – and without any love for yourself, how can you radiate confidence? Nurture your soul and gradually bring in a root chakra crystal, such as **black tourmaline** (see page 158), to ward off negative energies while you rediscover yourself and navigate these changes. This crystal is extremely grounding, ensuring you are in a place of stable energy as you start building yourself back up.

THE OWL

CRYSTAL GUIDE AND MOON KNOWLEDGE

POPULAR CRYSTALS DIRECTORY

Over the next few pages, you'll find information about popular crystals, including all the crystals featured elsewhere in this book. Use this directory as a reference guide, either to find out more about your crystal collection, or to find the perfect crystals to suit your needs based on their properties.

THE MOHS HARDNESS SCALE

This scale refers to the hardness and durability of the crystal, from 1 (very soft, like talc) to 10 (very hard, like diamond).

AGATE (GREY), *page 99*

Chakra: root
Mohs scale: 7
Associated flowers: lavender, peony
- Water-safe
- Gives strength and protection
- Grounds heightened energies
- Brings calm and balance

AGATE (PINK), *page 158*

Chakra: heart
Mohs scale: 7
Associated flowers: rose, sandalwood
- Water-safe
- Helps release and heal emotional issues
- Enhances concentration and analytical skills
- Boosts self-confidence
- Comforting and protective

AGATE (MOSS), *pages 62, 156*

Chakra: heart
Mohs scale: 6.5–7
Associated flowers: lavender, peppermint
- Water-safe
- Encourages a sense of tranquility
- Brings emotional balance
- Calms aggression
- Helps you connect to nature

AGATE (ZEBRA)/ZEBRA STONE

Chakra: root
Mohs scale: 6.5–7
Associated flowers: magnolia, rose
- Water-safe
- Increases stamina and energy levels
- Raises endurance
- Helps you accept love from those close to you

AMAZONITE, *page 90*

Chakra: heart
Mohs scale: 6–6.5
Associated flowers: geranium, lavender, rose
- Not water-safe
- Soothes the nervous system
- Helps you think rationally
- Helps heal past traumas
- Strengthens spiritual connections

AMBER, *page 158*

Chakra: Solar Plexus
Mohs scale: 2.5–3
Associated flowers: peace lily, bamboo
- Water-safe
- Absorbs negative energy
- Soothes and calms nerves
- Cleansing, energizing and lucky
- Helps ease pain when worn

AMBER ARAGONITE

Chakra: solar plexus/sacral
Mohs scale: 3–4
Associated flowers: daffodil, lavender
- Not water-safe
- Symbolizes truth and understanding
- Transforms geopathic stress
- Helps combat anger and stressful emotions
- Provides strength and support

AMETHYST, *pages 26, 77, 87, 115*

Chakra: crown/third eye
Mohs scale: 7
Associated flowers: lavender, jasmine
- Water-safe
- Reduces stress and anxiety
- Enhances meditation
- Emotionally calming and balancing
- Enhances psychic abilities

ANGELITE

Chakra: throat
Mohs scale: 3.5
Associated flowers: lotus flower, jasmine
- Not water-safe
- Transforms pain into healing and chaos into wholeness
- Creates a deep sense of inner peace
- Facilitates contact with spirit guides
- Enhances psychic abilities

APATITE

Chakra: throat
Mohs scale: 5
Associated flowers: begonia, marigold
- Not water-safe
- Clears confusion and frustration
- Expands knowledge and truth
- Eases sorrow, apathy and anger
- Boosts creativity and motivation

AQUAMARINE, *pages 41, 99*

Chakra: throat
Mohs scale: 7.5–8
Associated flowers: lavender, gladiolus
- Water-safe
- Calming and soothing
- Inspires truth, trust and letting go
- Invokes tolerance of others
- Supports in times of overwhelm

AVENTURINE (GREEN), *page 118*

Chakra: heart
Mohs scale: 6.5–7
Associated flowers: peony, rosemary, azalea
- Water-safe
- Attracts luck, abundance and success
- Instils a sense of emotional calm
- Helps when working through unresolved emotional issues

BLOODSTONE, *page 41*

Chakra: heart/root
Mohs scale: 6–7
Associated flowers: lavender, cactus
- Water-safe
- Balances the body to overcome any distress and anxiety
- Helps you face adversity head-on
- Helps protect against electromagnetic stresses

BRONZITE

Chakra: sacral/root
Mohs scale: 5.5
Associated flowers: bluebell, apple blossom
- Not water-safe
- Clears confusion and helps with decision-making
- Promotes peace and harmony
- Protective energy, cleansing areas of negativity

CALCITE (ORANGE), *pages 13, 102, 130*

Chakra: sacral
Mohs scale: 3
Associated flowers: yellow rose, rosemary, basil
- Not water-safe
- Brings sunshine, joy and alertness
- Raises good vibrations
- Strong energy-amplifier

CALCITE (PINK), *page 99*

Chakra: heart
Mohs scale: 3
Associated flowers: daffodil, rose
- Water-safe
- Evokes forgiveness
- Encourages love and kindness
- Connects the emotions to the intellect
- Unlocks creativity

CARNELIAN, *pages 13, 28, 51, 115*

Chakra: sacral
Mohs scale: 7
Associated flowers: rowan tree, black-eyed susan, marigold
- Water-safe
- Restores vitality and motivation
- Stimulates creativity
- Helps overcome emotional trauma
- Fertility booster

CELESTITE

Chakra: throat
Mohs scale: 3–3.5
Associated flowers: lotus flower
- Not water-safe
- Associated with the divine in meditation
- Facilitates contact with guardian angels
- Brings spiritually uplifting energies
- Promotes mindfulness

CHRYSOCOLLA, *page 139*

Chakra: throat/heart
Mohs scale: 2.5–3.5
Associated flowers: tulip, lilac, orchid
- Not water-safe
- Brings peace and tranquility
- Attracts unconditional love
- Helps you share your thoughts and feelings with others
- Connects you to your inner god(dess)

CITRINE, *pages 14, 62, 77, 115, 127, 139*

Chakra: solar plexus
Mohs scale: 7
Associated flowers: money plant, sunflower, lucky bamboo
- Water-safe
- Crystal of manifestation
- Raises self-esteem and confidence
- Brings joy and sunshine
- Attracts wealth and prosperity

EMERALD, *pages 61, 90, 139*

Chakra: heart
Mohs scale: 7.5–8
Associated flowers: aster, dahlia
- Not water-safe
- Life-affirming, enhancing inspiration
- Unlocks wisdom, balance and patience
- Helps to give and receive love

FLUORITE, *pages 14, 51, 62*

Chakra: third eye/heart
Mohs scale: 4
Associated flowers: lilac, lavender, white heather
- Not water-safe
- Neutralizes anxiety and stress
- Increases self-confidence
- Protective and stabilizing of all energies
- Helps you make secure decisions

FLUORITE (YELLOW)

Chakra: solar plexus
Mohs scale: 4
Associated flowers: amaryllis, marigold
• Not water-safe
• Fires up your intellect and creativity
• Improves logic and problem-solving
• Enhances a cooperative spirit
• Raises self-belief

GARNET (RED), *page 26*

Chakra: root
Mohs scale: 6.5–7.5
Associated flowers: basil, iris
• Not water-safe
• Balances and grounds energy
• Welcomes serenity or passion as appropriate
• Welcomes success and fortune, especially in business
• Helps you let go of old behaviours

HEMATITE, *page 87*

Chakra: root
Mohs scale: 5.5–6.5
Associated flowers: lemongrass, roses, sedum
• Not water-safe
• Brings calm in times of stress and worry
• Helps you stay emotionally grounded
• Turns negative energies into positive
• Stimulates concentration and focus

HEMIMORPHITE

Chakra: third eye/crown
Mohs scale: 4.5–5
Associated flower: lotus flower
• Not water-safe
• Raises healing abilities of all healers
• Enables better understanding and logical thinking
• Helps you detach from your ego and enhances spiritual growth

HOWLITE (WHITE)

Chakra: crown
Mohs scale: 3.5
Associated flowers: poppy, gerbera, daisy
• Not water-safe
• Links you to your higher consciousness
• Reduces anxiety, stress and tension
• Eases insomnia
• Creates self-awareness

IOLITE, *page 41*

Chakra: third eye/throat
Mohs scale: 7–7.5
Associated flowers: blue violet, lotus flower
• Not water-safe
• Enhances ability to have clear visions
• Promotes pure thoughts and intuition
• Improves self-acceptance
• Carries the spirit of journey and dreams

JADE, *pages 102, 158*

Chakra: heart
Mohs scale: 6.5–7
Associated flowers: peony, white heather
• Not water-safe
• Brings love and good luck
• Purifies the energies around you
• Protects loving energies from evils
• Dispels disaster

JASPER (RED), *pages 61, 77, 102, 118*

Chakra: root
Mohs scale: 6.5–7
Associated flowers: carnation, orchid
• Water-safe
• Renews strength and stamina
• Grounds energy to the earth
• Increases self-trust
• Promotes vitality and sexual vibrancy

JASPER (RED WINE)

Chakra: root/heart
Mohs scale: 6.5–7
Associated flowers: amaryllis, daffodil
- Water-safe
- Helps you stop holding yourself back
- Boosts your confidence
- Helps clear negative thoughts
- Strengthens personal power and peace

JASPER (YELLOW), *page 28*

Chakra: solar plexus
Mohs scale: 6.5–7
Associated flowers: achillea, sweet pea
- Water-safe
- Offers spiritual protection
- Good for protection during travel
- Facilitates positive communication
- Supports during times of stress

LABRADORITE, *pages 13, 52, 87, 156*

Chakra: third eye/throat
Mohs scale: 6–6.5
Associated flowers: lotus flower, white heather, gladiolus
- Not water-safe
- Awakens mystical and psychic abilities
- Creates a shield for auras
- Supportive in times of transformation
- Enhances willpower

LAPIS LAZULI, *pages 52, 62, 127*

Chakra: throat
Mohs scale: 5–6
Associated flowers: red poppy, rose, hydrangea
- Not water-safe
- The crystal of honour and power
- Enhances vision when making plans
- Promotes honesty, including to self
- Inspires confidence

MALACHITE, *page 139*

Chakra: throat/heart
Mohs scale: 3.5–4
Associated flowers: dahlia, lotus flower
- Not water-safe
- Creates balance
- Invites abundance to flow freely to you
- Casts a protective shield for your travels
- Absorbs anxiety and worries
- Instils good luck and protection

MOOKAITE, *page 127*

Chakra: root
Mohs scale: 6–7
Associated flowers: chamomile, lily
- Water-safe for short periods only
- Nurtures and supports during times of stress
- Welcomes peace and wholeness
- Helps you accept change
- Provides emotional growth

MOONSTONE, *pages 14, 61, 139, 156*

Chakra: sacral
Mohs scale: 6–6.5
Associated flowers: daffodil, orchid, hawthorn
- Water-safe
- Supports new beginnings
- Promotes inner growth and strength
- Enhances intuition and inspiration
- Supports fertility and menstrual cycles

MOONSTONE (PEACH), *page 28*

Chakras: crown/sacral
Mohs scale: 6–6.5
Associated flowers: tulips, sunflowers
- Not water-safe
- Helps you understand your emotions
- Illuminates visions and dreams
- Brings feelings of warmth and safety
- Encourages vulnerability in a safe space

MOONSTONE (RAINBOW), *pages 42, 156*

Chakra: crown/third eye/throat
Mohs scale: 6–6.5
Associated flowers: gladiolus, iris, white heather
• Water-safe
• Enhances mental power and agility
• Helps manage emotions
• Provides psychic protection
• Strengthens intuition

OBSIDIAN (BLACK), *page 130*

Chakra: root/third eye
Mohs scale: 5–6
Associated flowers: carnation, jasmine
• Water-safe
• A powerful cleanser of psychic smog
• Protects against attack
• Shields against negativity
• Grounds emotions
• Stimulates the gift of prophecy

ONYX (BLACK), *page 130*

Chakra: root
Mohs scale: 6.5–7
Associated flowers: snowdrop, magnolia
• Water-safe
• Powerfully protective
• Helps develop physical strength, stamina and self-control
• Imparts self-confidence
• Enhances wise decision-making

PREHNITE, *pages 51, 90*

Chakra: heart
Mohs scale: 6–6.5
Associated flowers: lavender, white heather, dahlia
• Not water-safe
• Stops you absorbing others' energy
• Offers protection, restoring wellbeing
• Brings inner peace and calm

PYRITE, *pages 77, 127*

Chakra: solar plexus
Mohs scale: 6–6.5
Associated flowers: iris, sunflower, rose
• Not water-safe
• Sparks creativity
• Promotes physical wellbeing
• Enhances willpower and strength
• Crystal of luck and abundance

QUARTZ (CLEAR), *pages 14, 26, 42, 51, 118, 139*

Chakra: crown
Mohs scale: 7
Associated flowers: carnation, foxglove, rose
• Water-safe
• Master healer
• Amplifies energies from other crystals
• Can be programmed with intentions
• Clears the mind of negativity

QUARTZ (FIRE/HEMATOID)

Chakra: sacral
Mohs scale: 7
Associated flowers: hydrangea, acacia blossom
• Water-safe
• Balances mind, body and spirit
• Transforms negative to positive energy
• Shines love into any space

QUARTZ (GOLDEN HEALER)

Chakra: crown
Mohs scale: 7
Associated flowers: alstroemeria, lotus flower
• Water-safe
• Enters the crown chakra and surrounds the aura with golden light
• Restores the body's natural balance
• Attracts success and abundance

QUARTZ (ROSE), *pages 14, 26, 52, 118, 130, 158*

Chakra: heart
Mohs scale: 7
Associated flowers: carnation, violet, sunflower
- Water-safe
- The crystal of universal love
- Restores harmony in relationships
- Promotes deep inner healing
- Supports fertility

QUARTZ (RUTILATED)

Chakra: solar plexus
Mohs scale: 7
Associated flowers: gladiolus, lotus flower
- Water-safe
- Helps you let go of the past
- Protects against others' ill thoughts
- Brings physical and mental balance

QUARTZ (SMOKY), *pages 62, 130*

Chakra: root
Mohs scale: 7
Associated flowers: lavender, violet
- Water-safe
- Connects you to nature
- Helps you reconnect with the earth
- Gently neutralizes negative vibrations
- Relieves stress and anxiety

RHODONITE, *pages 28, 99*

Chakra: heart
Mohs scale: 5.5–6.5
Associated flowers: allium, chrysanthemum
- Not water-safe
- Attracts the right people for success
- Contains a nurturing, supportive energy
- Heals emotional shock and heartache
- Helps you realize your full potential

SARDONYX

Chakra: root
Mohs scale: 6.5
Associated flowers: yellow rose, lucky bamboo, poppy
- Water-safe
- Protects and builds courage
- Attracts stable friendships
- Brings lasting happiness and luck
- Promotes clear communication

SEFTONITE

Chakra: root
Mohs scale: 6
Associated flowers: money plant, jade plant, jasmine
- Not water-safe
- Banishes evil and negativity
- Brings mental calm and clarity
- Gives deep-rooted courage
- Attracts wealth

SELENITE, *page 42*

Chakra: crown/third eye
Mohs scale: 2
Associated flowers: snowdrop, violet, lavender, lotus flower
- Not water-safe
- Channels energy from the cosmos and universe, delivering it to Earth
- Helps access angelic consciousness
- Helps you think without prejudice

SELENITE (ORANGE)

Chakra: sacral
Mohs scale: 2
Associated flowers: orchid, jade plant
- Not water-safe
- Brings luck and protective energies
- Encourages connection with the divine
- Calms and enhances a meditative state
- Enhances fertility

SODALITE, *pages 87, 102, 158*

Chakra: throat
Mohs scale: 5.5–6
Associated flower: daffodil
• Not water-safe
• Improves intuition and rational thought
• Emotionally calming
• Encourages communication and helps you verbalize your feelings

SUNSTONE, *pages 52, 115*

Chakra: sacral
Mohs scale: 6.5–7.2
Associated flowers: lotus, peonies
• Water-safe for short periods only
• Welcomes abundance and joy
• Attracts good things, like a magnet
• Emotionally empowering
• Lifts your confidence

TIGER'S EYE, *pages 42, 61, 77, 90*

Chakra: solar plexus/sacral
Mohs scale: 6.5–7
Associated flowers: peony, peppermint, jasmine
• Water-safe
• Brings protection and good luck
• Promotes mental clarity
• Dispels fear and anxiety
• Inspires creativity and good judgement

TIGER'S EYE (RED), *pages 13, 28, 158*

Chakra: root
Mohs scale: 6.5–7
Associated flowers: white carnation, yellow poppy
• Water-safe
• Keeps your energy grounded
• Draws positive, nurturing energy to you
• Helps you manifest your dreams
• Enhances confidence and self-esteem

TOURMALINE (BLACK), *pages 28, 42, 77, 118, 127, 158*

Chakra: root
Mohs scale: 7–7.5
Associated flowers: rowan tree, peace lily, chrysanthemum
• Not water-safe
• Highly protective
• Grounds and balances body and mind
• Cleanses negative thoughts
• Detoxifies the environment

TOURMALINE (PINK), *page 62*

Chakra: heart
Mohs scale: 7–7.5
Associated flowers: calendula, chrysanthemum
• Not water-safe
• Cleanses destructive emotions
• Releases guilt, worry and anxieties
• Helps soothe insomnia

TURQUOISE, *page 41*

Chakra: throat
Mohs scale: 5–6
Associated flowers: foxglove, pink hyacinth
• Not water-safe
• Brings luck, peace and protection
• Allows love and communication to flow
• Awakens creativity and honesty
• Cleanses negativity away

UNAKITE, *page 90*

Chakra: heart
Mohs scale: 6–7
Associated flowers: orchid, lotus flower
• Not water-safe
• Resonates with the frequencies of love, compassion and kindness
• Balances the emotional body
• Carries a nurturing energy

CHOOSING CRYSTALS

It may appear that there are lots of different factors to think about when choosing a crystal, but just remember: it's all about intuition.

COLOURS

Colours themselves have so much energy and meaning, and can change the whole tone of a room. We spend so much time choosing a colour scheme for our home, and we each have favourite colours that we wear. But what is it about these colours that makes us choose them? Our subconscious craves certain feelings, and our emotional health has particular needs, and these can be linked to the colours we are drawn to.

When reading through the next few pages, think back to why you chose that particular paint, top, dress, car or bag. The simple reason of 'just liking it' may run deeper than you think.

What are your go-to colours? Do the meanings below resonate with you?

PURPLE

The majestic purple is a powerful colour. It is a symbol of royalty, but also strength. It boosts confidence and ambition, deflecting negativity while offering emotional stability.

Popular crystals in this shade include **amethyst** (page 166) and **fluorite** (page 167), two great crystals to have around in times of stress and anxiety.

WHITE

The beautiful serene colour of white is a symbol of purity and angels. It symbolizes the start of new beginnings and wiping the slate clean. It is calming and soothing, yet clinical, ideal for those who feel angry and want a sense of calm.

White crystals, particularly **howlite** (page 168), are wonderful for helping you get to sleep. See also **quartz** (pages 170–171) and **moonstone** (page 169).

BLUE

Just like white, blue evokes serenity and calm. Like the ocean, it gently envelops you, wrapping you in an emotional hug. It brings a sense of confidence and stability, and has a positive effect on the mind.

Keep **sodalite** (page 172) around, especially during exams, studying and difficult conversations. It will keep you level-headed.

GREEN

This beautiful fresh tone symbolizes new beginnings and positive change. It gives a healthy energy that will work in line with your own to help you take on new challenges with positivity.

Green is a famously lucky colour, and **jade** (page 168) is a wonderful stone to have around as a lucky charm.

YELLOW

The colour of sunshine, calm, hope and happiness, yellow brings joy and energy to any space. It is the perfect choice if you are looking to attract abundance into your life and a surge of positivity.

Citrine (page 167) is a popular choice, as it lifts your spirits like a summer's day.

ORANGE

The colour of vitality and flamboyance: a combination of red and yellow, red's fierceness is toned down by yellow's hopeful energy to create this vibrant colour.

Orange **carnelian** (page 167) gently stimulates a burst of energy and restores your vitality.

RED

The colour of passion, red also symbolizes adventure. It is a good colour to have around if you wish to capture attention, elicit emotion, and convey confidence.

Red goldstone, a man-made crystal, evokes all of these things. The copper within the crystal works with the red to spark confidence while protecting against anxieties.

PINK

Pink, the colour of love and security, is like a warm hug of kindness. Not only does it project love outwardly, attracting good relationships and friendship, it also encourages self-love and loyalty.

The most popular pink crystal is **rose quartz** (page 171), attracting love and wholesome friendships to you.

BLACK

Black is a powerful and elegant colour. Black crystals are highly protective against negativity and dark energies. They can be used for protection during travel, as well as in the home: placing them by the front door wards off evil and negative emotions.

When carried with you, black crystals ground your energies to ensure that you can't be affected by external factors. They are like guardian angels in crystal form.

SHAPES

There's no limit to the shapes and sizes a crystal can naturally grow into: this depends on the conditions in which they grow, in a process that can take thousands of years. Once mined, crystals are shaped by human hands and take on symbolic meanings: choose a shape that will amplify your experience.

CUBES

Use a cube-shaped crystal during meditation or display one in the home to help ground your energies and connect you with the earth. The cube is a protective shape, and by placing it in a corner, you can keep any space, such as your home, safe.

PYRAMIDS

The pyramid is an incredible generator of energy: this beautiful shape has a strong base, anchoring your intention or desires, while reaching upwards to catapult them out into the universe and beyond. Whatever you want to attract, pyramids will level up your life.

SPHERES

Holding a spherical crystal keeps you grounded, giving you insight without the need to enter a deep, meditative state, keeping you connected to the energy surrounding you. Holding a sphere is truly special, like holding the whole world in your hand.

TUMBLED STONES

The 'humble tumble' is the perfect starter crystal. Small but mighty, it gives you a taster of a particular crystal before you commit to a larger piece. Keep discreetly in your pocket in times of need.

CRYSTAL POINTS

Use these around the new moon to help you manifest and create. All that energy floods out into your room – and the universe – enriching your surroundings and working to generate your desires and dreams.

HEARTS

These hand-cut crystals carry loving energy, attract forgiveness and light, and help you both to receive love and to love yourself more. Heart-shaped stones can be used in meditation to fill your heart with love, or to support you as you cleanse old wounds and traumas. A perfect healing stone.

CLUSTERS

There is nothing quite so mystical as a group of natural crystal points. Perfect for creating harmony, try displaying one on your dining table or a coffee table at home, or, to promote dialogue at work, place one in a conference room or other communal space.

CRYSTAL MAINTENANCE AND CARE

CLEANSING AND CHARGING YOUR CRYSTALS

It is important to cleanse and charge your crystals at least once a month to make sure they're zinging with energy at all times. Just as you would charge your phone or car battery, or care for yourself in order to recharge, crystals need to be 'fed' good energies so that they can tune in to yours. When you are calling upon a particular crystal to help you through a time of heightened energy, such as stressful exams, ill health or a relationship break-up, it is recommended that you cleanse and charge your crystals more often – weekly or even nightly. If you have bought crystals from a store or a source that doesn't keep them away from external energies, it is also recommended you cleanse and charge them for your own use upon receiving them.

Here are some methods for cleansing and charging.

SELENITE

Selenite purifies, cleanses and charges all crystals placed on or around it. Selenite is a self-generating crystal, meaning there is no need to cleanse or charge it, so it's very useful to have in your collection. Place your crystals with the selenite for four to eight hours, or ideally overnight, and they will be like just like new.

SUNSHINE

Place your crystals in the sunshine for up to four hours. The sunlight will burn off any old or stored energy. Any longer, and you may find that your crystals fade a little.

FULL MOON

Bathing your crystals in moonlight is one of the most popular and widely known cleansing and charging methods. Simply place your crystals in a spot where the moonlight will reach them, and let the moon's energy work its divine magic. It is very possible you will feel a 'zing' when you gather your crystals the next day, as your crystals will be radiating and harnessing all that lunar energy. If you are placing the crystals outside, check the Popular Crystals Directory (pages 165–172) or the list on page 180 to see if they are water-safe. If not, place them in a glass-lidded dish to protect them from the rain.

COMMON SAGE

Sage comes in a variety of colours, types, bundles and sticks, but I personally love using a sage bundle or a sage incense stick to cleanse my crystals. Light the sage, then waft to carry away any stored energies.

This is especially good for removing negative energies, and has the added bonus of resetting the energy within your space and your aura as well. Such a clever plant!

When choosing sage, please do ensure it has been ethically grown, sourced and sold, just as you do with your crystals.

SOUND

Drums, gongs, singing bowls and meditative music can do so much more than evoking relaxation and meditation. Those karmic soundwaves can break up stored energies within your crystals and carry them away. So next time you are practising, place your crystals close by and create twice the magic.

EARTH/SOIL

Gardening just got a whole lot more fun! Reserve a space in your garden for your crystals, making sure you mark it clearly so you don't lose them. Check the Popular Crystals Directory (pages 165–172) or the list on page 180 to make sure you only use this method for water-safe crystals, in case it rains. Place the crystals in the earth, about 2.5cm/1 inch down, and leave them for a minimum of 12 hours so they can renew and regenerate their energy. To many, this is the most organic method of cleansing, as you are momentarily returning them to the earth that created them.

FRESH WATER

Simply run water-safe crystals (see the Popular Crystals Directory on pages 165–172 or the list on page 180) under clear, fresh water from a natural source, such as a stream, then dry them thoroughly.

SALT WATER

Mix 1 tablespoon of sea salt into a bowl of water and place water-safe crystals in the bowl for up to 48 hours. See the Popular Crystals Directory on pages 165–172 or the list on page 180 to check whether your crystals are water-safe.

PROGRAMMING CRYSTALS AND SETTING INTENTIONS

While crystals harness their own powers and energies, it is important to give them an idea of the kind of support you would like to receive from them. After every cleanse – or when you first receive the crystal – hold it in your hands and either say out loud or visualize in your mind's eye what it is that you would like. You can be specific, naming a certain timeframe, or leave it open-ended. Have fun, don't be afraid to ask for something too big, and truly believe that you deserve everything you ask for. The universe can sense any doubts, so send out positive thoughts and visualize yourself receiving what it is that you desire.

Once you have expressed your desire to the crystal, thank it for bringing your desire to you. Act as if you already have it. Keep your crystal in your pocket or bag if you need its support when out and about, or place it in the room where that support is most needed, whether at home or at work.

The important thing is to have fun and be kind. This isn't a tool for manifesting negative energy against others. Always remember karma is at play. Creating dark energy or ill-feeling towards others could create a negative rebound towards you. Be kind, always.

STORING YOUR CRYSTALS

If you are putting your crystals away to 'sleep' when you do not need them, I recommend placing them in a dark wooden box, or any box made from natural materials, with a piece of selenite and some lavender sprinkled inside. Your crystals' energies will rest better in a natural box, and the selenite will keep them vibrating and ready for a new intention to be set at a moment's notice. The dried lavender, meanwhile, protects the crystals, absorbing any energies that may not be so welcome. It is not essential, however, so don't worry if you don't have any or can't use it due to allergies.

If your collection is small, an organza or velvet bag with a small piece of lavender is ideal: the soft material will not scratch your crystals, and they can still 'breathe' within the bag.

DISPLAYING YOUR CRYSTALS

A popular option for storing and displaying your crystals is to place them in a selenite bowl for its ability to keep their energies vibrating.

There are a few things to consider when displaying your crystals.

SUNLIGHT

Crystals such as **amethyst, carnelian** and **citrine** will eventually fade in sunlight, so it's best to restrict their time in sunny spots to no more than four hours a day.

AIR

Crystals that contain metals or iron will oxidize or rust when kept out in the open over time. These include **pyrite, hematite** and **red tiger's eye**.

WATER

Some crystals are porous or salt-based, such as selenite. These will break down and dissolve in water or wet environments over time. See the Popular Crystals Directory (page 165–172) or the list on page 180 to check if a particular crystal is water-safe.

CONFLICTING ENERGIES

When creating your crystal displays, or when choosing which stones to wear or carry, it's important to choose crystals that complement each other. Placing a crystal that calms you alongside one that energizes you will effectively cancel out the energies of both crystals. While it's lovely to choose crystals that work well with your décor, it's also key to choose pieces that will create the right energy and support for what you need.

When starting a collection, it's near impossible to remember the name and properties of each crystal. Store your crystals with an identification card – you'll thank me later!

THE ELEMENTS

The elements are used to categorize zodiac signs and are symbolized in rituals using candles and crystals in the corresponding colours.

EARTH

- **Colours:** Brown, green, dark orange
- **Direction:** North

AIR

- **Colours:** White, yellow, dark blue
- **Direction:** East

FIRE

- **Colours:** Red, orange, gold
- **Direction:** South

WATER

- **Colours:** Blue, green
- **Direction:** West

POPULAR WATER-SAFE AND NON-WATER-SAFE CRYSTALS

Use this as a quick reference guide, or head to the directory starting on page 165 for information on specific crystals.

WATER-SAFE CRYSTALS

- Rose quartz
- Amethyst
- Citrine
- Black obsidian
- Blue obsidian
- Clear quartz
- Carnelian
- Agate
- Amber
- Jasper
- Smoky quartz
- Onyx
- Green aventurine

NON-WATER-SAFE CRYSTALS

These crystals tend to be soft, and with frequent exposure to moisture will absorb tiny amounts of water. Some contain metals and will eventually rust.

- Fluorite
- Selenite
- Lepidolite
- Opalite
- Malachite
- Turquoise
- Pyrite
- Angelite
- Hematite
- Apatite
- Rhodonite

WHY DID MY CRYSTAL BREAK?

It's never a nice feeling when a crystal you've brought into your life suddenly cracks, breaks or vanishes without a trace. Considered by many to be a bad omen, this can, understandably, scare the owner. However, there's no need to worry.

Think of your crystals as a metaphysical sponge. They work hard to support you or your environment, meaning they come into constant contact with energies from various sources. They'll eventually reach their peak and not be able to absorb any more external energy, or indeed radiate to their full capacity. Like a balloon, they'll go pop! Their energy shatters the crystal's vessel as it explodes out to escape.

How can you stop this from happening? If you're going through a time of heightened stress, worry, love or a busy time at work, it's important to pay your crystals a little extra attention and cleanse them as often as you can (see page 176) – try cleansing overnight with selenite. However, if you're not going through a high-energy period, a crystal breaking may simply be a sign that it has served its purpose. Let it rest for at least 30 days and, if you feel that you want to gift all or a piece of the breakage to loved ones, use your intuition to decide who could benefit from its support. You'll know if you're ready to let it go, especially if the area of your life you were using the crystal for has improved. Want to keep it? That's OK. Rest it for 30 days, charge it and give it new intentions.

If you lose a crystal, it's no doubt served its purpose for you. It will reappear when you need it the most.

CREATING YOUR ALTAR

An altar is a place of power and spiritual and supernatural strength within your home or garden. Whatever your beliefs, an altar offers a great space for focus, comfort, wisdom and calm. But how do you create one? A common theme here, much of this is down to the power of intuition – you may even have created one without realizing. That space on your sideboard, fireplace or desk filled with items that make you smile when you walk past? That is a positive energy altar. If you need a little guidance, the following steps can help you.

1. Choose a space. Decide whether you want the altar to feature in a family space or act as an area for private contemplation and spirituality in the room you use the most, like your bedroom.

2. Gather tools and objects for your altar. Use your intuition, unless you are following a specific ritual, spell or spiritual path that dictates what to use. Popular items for altars include your crystals (see more on displaying your crystals on page 179), candles, written intentions, flowers, statues or symbolic tokens, photos of your ancestors, images of items you wish to manifest, books and incense. Remember, this is your altar, and it embodies who and what you are.

3. Once you have chosen your space, cleanse it – physically and spiritually, using a natural cleaner, such as a one that is citrus-based, and a sage-based incense to smoke the area.

4. Place your selected items with care, and ensure your surfaces will be protected from wax, ash and pollen. When arranging your altar items, it is important to make sure they are all visible. Placing the larger and taller items at the back will allow each one to be seen and to be receptive of your intentions and spiritual work.

5. To get the most from your altar, interact with it as regularly as you can, but once a season is fine if you find it too intense. You could change the decorations each season to reflect the time of the year.

6. You may just wish to use the altar as a positive energy generator or as a space to read your tarot or oracle cards with clarity. You can also use it to prepare and set your intentions, especially on a new moon for extra power (see the new moon ritual on page 187). As you receive your intentions, give thanks to the altar and bury or burn the paper as an offering.

CANDLE COLOURS AND THEIR MEANINGS

When you are creating an altar or working on spells, or if you simply want to evoke a certain energy in your home, the colour of the candles you choose can make a big difference.

· **White:** Purity, new beginnings, protection, serenity, peace

· **Gold:** Wealth, success, motivation, enlightenment, manifestation

· **Orange:** Celebration, joy, intellect, energy, stamina

· **Yellow:** Focus, confidence, wisdom, logic, clarity, happiness

· **Green:** Money, success, opportunity, prosperity, growth, health

· **Blue:** Communication, good fortune, wisdom, peace, forgiveness

Purple: Spiritual enlightenment, magic, Intuition, meditation

· **Pink:** Romance, love, friendship, self-appreciation and self-love, happiness

· **Red:** Passion, stamina, endurance, courage, willpower

· **Black:** Protection from negative energy and ill feelings

A LITTLE MOON KNOWLEDGE

The moon is a source of wonder and is responsible for the seasons, thanks to the moon's gravitational pull on the Earth, as well as the tides. In short, it creates the basic rhythms of life.

Such a magical astrological wonder has been worshipped for thousands of years, and many mythologies feature moon goddesses, including Selene (Greek), Luna (Roman) and Change'e (Chinese). But where does the moon feature in modern-day magic?

THE MOON'S PHASES

The full lunar cycle lasts approximately 29 days, and sees the moon waxing (growing larger) and waning (growing smaller) as the cycle progresses. The moon is called upon in rituals throughout the month, most notably at the full moon or new moon, but each phase has a specific energy.

New moon: A good time for new beginnings and starting new projects

Waxing crescent: Positive actions are encouraged and rewarded

First quarter: A period for strength, determination and commitment to action

Waxing gibbous: A time to strive to complete your projects

Full moon: Represents completion, fertility, abundance and transformation

Waning gibbous: A time for ridding yourself of bad habits, stresses and negative thoughts

Third quarter: Use your intuition and spiritual understanding to let go that which no longer serves you

Waning crescent: Restore your thoughts and your positive intentions

New moon: Back to the start of the cycle

THE NEW MOON

The new moon is the start of the cycle, but is often overlooked by those who are unfamiliar with the moon's phases. However, it is arguably the most important and most powerful time for manifesting. The new moon is a symbol of new beginnings, fresh starts and setting powerful intentions that you want to receive by the time of the full moon – in other words, a time for dreaming big.

Each lunar cycle is a rebirth, with endless opportunities opening up in front of you, so this is the best time to start an exciting new project or make new plans.

If you look up to the sky, you'll see a slight line of light around a dark moon. This amazing sight is caused by the sun, moon and Earth being in an almost perfect line.

NEW MOON RITUAL

Below is my personal new moon ritual. I suggest using **moonstone** for a positive new start and **citrine** for joy, energy and abundance – though you can always use your favourite crystals or a crystal that ties in with the specific manifestation you are working on. For example, if you are manifesting a new relationship, you might decide to use **rose quartz**.

1. Take a bath or shower to wash away your worries and any old energies that are no longer needed.

2. Set up an area that won't be disturbed. Light a candle and choose some flowers and crystals. Look at the flowers recommended for each month for suggestions.

3. Calm and slow down your mind so you can focus better. Concentrate on your breathing and relax and meditate for at least 10 minutes.

4. Cleanse away stagnant energies throughout your home, using fresh air, incense or ethically sourced sage. Visualize the old energies leaving your space.

5. Write down your intentions and place the piece of paper under a powerful manifesting crystal, such as **clear quartz** or **citrine**.

6. Leave the space or altar in place, and revisit it to give thanks at the next full moon, in about 14 days.

THE FULL MOON

The full moon symbolizes the peak of the cycle, the realization of your dreams and desires. It's about being grateful for what you have and reflecting on your progress, celebrating how far you've come.

The full moon looks exactly as described: full. A beautiful ball of light that might be a silvery white or an orangey-red depending on the time of year. There are an abundance of amazing rituals you can conduct on the full moon: here are just a few.

MOON WATER RITUAL

Cleanse a glass container or bottle using filtered water or a cleansing smoke, such as ethically sourced sage. Fill it with drinking water and a quartz family crystal (see pages 170–171), if you like, and leave to charge under the light of the moon. It can then be used in spellwork, rituals, or even in the bath or for watering your plants – anywhere you want to add a sprinkle of magic.

TAROT

If you use tarot as part of your craft, the full moon is a good time to consult your deck for clarity, guidance and answers. If you have an affirmation or angel deck, this is perfectly fine to use instead.

CLEANSE YOUR CRYSTALS

Place your crystals under the light of the full moon to cleanse them (see page 176).

GRATITUDE RITUAL

Take some time on the night of the full moon to reflect on what you're thankful for in your life. Write it down to revisit later.

RECEIVING RITUAL

This ritual is the second part of the new moon ritual on page 187. Light a candle in the same colour as the one you used at the new moon. This welcomes the element of fire to ignite your intentions and goals. Take out your new moon intentions and use the candle to set the paper alight. Drop the burning paper into a fireproof bowl and let it burn, showing your readiness to receive. Let the candle burn out, then bury the ashes and candle.

THE SUPERMOON

A supermoon is a full moon, but with extra oomph! I will always remember September 1997, when I experienced my first supermoon. There are only three of four in a year, so I felt blessed to see the Harvest Moon – already large, when not a supermoon – at just the right moment. I was driving, and as I turned down a road near my home, there it was, right in front of me, hanging above the road as if it was going to touch it. In terms of size, the moon span was wider than the road, and its colour was a vivid burned orange.

Can you recall seeing your first supermoon? If you're yet to enjoy this spectacle, make a note in your calendar to look out for the next one.

The supermoon amplifies and heightens energy. Your raw emotions will be felt even more strongly, and you'll receive extra luck if you ask for it. It's a time for growth, change, adaptability and fertility.

THE BLUE MOON

Have you ever heard the saying 'once in a blue moon'? This is because the blue moon is extra special and rare. Every few years, the moon completes its final cycle about 11 days before the Earth finishes its orbit around the sun. This means that that year, there's an extra full moon: the blue moon. The origin of the name is uncertain, but it's used to describe a second full moon within a calendar month.

THE POWER OF THE MOON

Many fear the moon, but as I hope you have learned here, it has so much to give and can bring real enrichment to your life. Use the moon wisely to invite abundance and manifest your dreams into existence. There are so many beautiful courses, books and websites (see Resources on page 190) out there that will help you learn more about the moon, so happy discovering!

RESOURCES

Wiccan Feasts, Celebrations & Rituals, Silja, Cico Books (2021)

The Ultimate Guide to Chakras, Athena Perrakis, Fair Winds Press (2018)

The Old Farmer's Almanac, HarperCollins (annual)

The Crystal Bar website and online store *https://www.thecrystalbar.co.uk/*

The Crystal Bar Instagram @the_crystal_bar

Up Helly Aa official website *https://www.uphellyaa.org/*

Earth Hour official website *https://www.wwf.org.uk/earth-hour*

GLOSSARY OF TERMS

Cosmos: The universe as a whole.

Chakras: Originating in India and first mentioned in the *Vedas*, the chakras form part of an energy system flowing from the base of your spine to your head. There are popularly believed to be 7 chakras: root, sacral, solar plexus, heart, throat, third eye and crown. See above for resources.

Deity: A god, goddess or someone with divine status, quality or nature.

Mohs hardness scale: A scale that refers to the hardness and durability of the crystal, with 10 being the hardest and 1 being the softest.

Pagan: A person holding religious beliefs other than the main world religions. Pagans believe that nature is sacred, and the natural cycles of birth, growth and death are profoundly spiritual.

Pentagram: A five-pointed star that protects against evil spirits.

Sigil: An inscribed or painted symbol with a magical meaning.

Smudge wand: Used for healing, ceremonial and energy-clearing work.

Triple goddess: A deity celebrated and revered in many spiritual traditions.

Triple moon: The symbol of the waxing, full and waning moon represents aspects of the maiden, mother and crone. Each symbolizes a separate stage in the female life cycle and often rules one of the realms of heavens, earth and underworld.

Universe: The universe in spirituality is a high vibrational energetic being that exists behind the psychic realm.

Managing Director Sarah Lavelle
Assistant Editor Sofie Shearman
Head of Design Claire Rochford
Photographer India Hobson
Illustrator Anastasia Stefurak
Head of Production Stephen Lang
Senior Production Controller
  Sabeena Atchia

Published in 2023 by Quadrille,
an imprint of Hardie Grant Publishing

Quadrille
52–54 Southwark Street
London SE1 1UN
quadrille.com

Text © Claire Titmus 2023
Illustrations © Anastasia Stefurak 2023
Photography © India Hobson 2023
Compilation, design and layout
© Quadrille 2023

Cataloguing in Publication Data: a catalogue
record for this book is available from the British
Library.

ISBN 978 1 78713 014 5

Printed in China

The information in this book is not intended to
constitute or replace genuine medical advice.
The reader should always consult a medical
professional in matters relating to their health
and wellbeing, both physical and mental.

ACKNOWLEDGEMENTS

Special thanks to my wonderful editor Sofie Shearman for supporting, guiding, empowering and believing in me at every step. To Quadrille for the vision to bring such knowledge to the world, and the extremely talented photographer India Hobson, illustrator Anastasia Stefurak and designer Claire Rochford for bringing the words to life in a beautifully enchanting way.

Thank you to the incredibly talented mystics and healers that have empowered me to believe in and grow my healing wisdom. To those who trust in me to help empower their lives and take time to pass on their learnings to future generations – keep believing in who you are and stay true to you, always.

Finally, to my loved ones and friends, especially my husband Stuart, for supporting me in many beautiful ways while travelling my new path of destiny – this is all for you.

ABOUT THE AUTHOR

Claire Titmus is a certified Advanced Crystal Healer and the founder of The Crystal Bar, an online store dedicated to ethically sourced crystals and mystical items. Far from just showcasing her own products, Claire uses her social media channels to share daily crystal wisdom, moon knowledge and messages of the day, alongside teaching her followers about the properties and uses of different crystals.

A NOTE ON THE SEASONS

This book follows the cycle of the year in the Northern Hemisphere. The seasons in the Northern Hemisphere are defined as follows:

Spring: March, April, May

Summer: June, July, August

Autumn: September, October, November

Winter: December, January, February